PETER SPENCER
The Florida State University

PETER M. TEMKO
The University of Tennessee at Chattanooga

a practical approach to the study of form in music

WAVELAND
PRESS, INC.
Prospect Heights, Illinois

For information about this book, write or call:

Waveland Press, Inc.
P.O. Box 400
Prospect Heights, Illinois 60070
(708) 634-0081

contents

preface

This text is intended for the undergraduate college-level musician who has had little, if any, training in the perception of form in music. Because, however, the effective presentation of the subject matter would be virtually impossible without a certain amount of formal training on the part of the reader, the authors assume that the student has a working knowledge of traditional cadences, of diatonic and chromatic harmony, and of common terminology as it pertains to tempo, dynamics, and expression marks. In some programs, the book could be used profitably by sophomores; in programs that introduce chromatic harmony in the second year, it properly belongs as a text for an upper-division form course.

The study of form in college-level music courses is generally hindered by one basic misconception. It is thought that, unlike any other attribute of music that musicians consider, form is a topic of visual study. It is forgotten that form, or structure, is an attribute that grows from the music itself; thus, it should be perceived aurally as the music progresses in the same manner that other musical attributes are perceived. The study of form, then, should be an exercise in the perception of the interaction of a number of discrete musical events and should embody much more than a search for visual cues.

The basic purpose of this text, therefore, is to provide students of form with perceptual tools that allow them to proceed from the aural experience to an understanding of the arch-principles upon which music is organized.

The perception of structure relies on the practiced recognition of musical events that signal to the listener important points in the music's design. The identification of these "structural phenomena" allows the listener to divide the larger musical entity into manageable sections that provide information about its organization. Thus, the principles by which a given piece of music is organized may be gleaned from paying attention to the internal attributes that give a section its specific identity, to the functional relations between sections, and to the ordering of those sections. *All* this information is available from listening to the music.

The authors believe the analytical tools that the first three chapters of this text are designed to exercise provide a way in which students may discover the organization of any piece of music from the perception of audible musical events. The second part of the text is restricted to a discussion of music that illustrates basic formal principles. A thorough grasp of these tools and principles, however, will help to clarify the perception of the designs of the many pieces of music whose structures fall outside the scope of this text.

This book is not a reference tool regarding genre and style. Information of this kind may be found in the anthologies to which most of the exercises are keyed. They are Mary Wennerstrom's *Anthology of Musical Structure and Style* (Englewood Cliffs, N.J.: Prentice-Hall, 1983), Charles Burkhart's *Anthology for Musical Analysis,* fourth edition (New York: Holt, Rinehart and Winston, Inc., 1986), Ralph Turek's *Analytical Anthology of Music* (New York: Knopf, 1984), and Roger Kamien's *The Norton Scores,* fourth edition expanded (New York: W. W. Norton & Co., Inc., 1984).

While much of the analytical work in this text might be done profitably without hearing the music, the authors feel strongly that, whenever possible, multiple performances of the examples and exercises should be provided. Every effort has been made to choose music from the anthologies that is easily accessible from the keyboard or from readily available recordings. In addition, supplementary exercise material, which can be found in most score and record collections, has been suggested from outside the anthologies.

In summation, this text, while intended for undergraduate music students, serves the needs of all functioning musicians whose aim is the communication of music to others. The authors believe that the understanding of musical form based upon the systematic perception of musical phenomena is fundamental to that communication.

P.S.
P.M.T.

1

structural phenomena

INTRODUCTION

A musical composition is the result of a process by which complete structures are built from smaller units. On an obvious level, a symphony is typically organized in several discrete units called movements. The organization of smaller pieces without such obvious divisions is the result of the same process. The understanding of a complex musical entity, therefore, depends upon the understanding of relationships between smaller units within that entity. Such an understanding is dependent upon locating those points at which the larger structure is divided into smaller sections. Thus, the first analytical tool in the task of formal perception is the development of a sensitivity to those musical phenomena that help identify those points. These *structural phenomena* are discussed in this chapter.

Phenomena

Structural phenomena are cues, perceived both aurally and visually, that allow the larger structure to be understood in smaller sections. These phenomena are associated with the following common musical elements: *cadence, tonality, tempo, meter, rhythm, dynamics, density, timbre, register, texture,* and *motive*.

What follows defines each of the elements and illustrates the phenomena associated with them.

Cadence.   As a structural phenomenon, cadence is understood as a *point of relative cessation of musical activity.* Such cessation of activity may signal the reaching of an important harmonic or melodic goal, or it may simply represent a relaxation of rhythmic activity. In some contexts, one of these components may be more significant than others. For purposes of formal perception, however, the *sensation* of the music's having reached a point of cadence is more important than the identification of the components that produce the cadence. It is that sensation which produces a *structural phenomenon.*

Examples 1.1–1.4 illustrate cadence as a structural phenomenon. Note the harmonic, melodic, or rhythmic components in each case.

Example 1.1   Beethoven: Sonata in E major, Op. 14, No. 1, I, mm. 1–6

The sensation of cadence is particularly strong in m. 4 of Example 1.1. Harmonic, melodic, and rhythmic factors all contribute to the perception of the phenomenon.

NOTE

1.   The authentic close occurs over a tonic pedal.
2.   The melody reaches its goal at the beginning of the third beat.
3.   The rhythmic activity comes to a complete halt.

Example 1.2   J. S. Bach: *Well-Tempered Clavier (W.T.C.), Vol. I, Fugue 16 in
G minor, mm. 1–12*

   While harmonic cadential activity may be perceived at several points
in Example 1.2, the first convincing structural cadence occurs in the tonic
key on the third quarter note of m. 10. The continuation, however, of the
melodic and rhythmic activity, accompanied by modulation to the relative
major, leads to a stronger cadence on the downbeat of m. 12.

NOTE

1. The bass movement in m. 10 produces a more convincing authentic cadence
in the tonic key than those heard previously.
2. The strength of the cadence in m. 12 is enhanced by the vi-ii-V-I harmonic
progression that precedes it.

Example 1.3 Schumann: *Album for the Young*, Op. 68, No. 14, "Kleine Studie," mm. 1–20

In Example 1.3, harmonic activity alone produces the cadential sensation on the downbeat of m. 17. In spite of the persistence of the rhythm and the absence of any obvious melody, the harmonic progression ii-ii$^6_5$-V7-V+ ensures that the tonic chord that follows is heard as a structural cadential point.

NOTE

A weak authentic cadence over a tonic pedal may be perceived in m. 4.

Example 1.4 Paul Hindemith: "Interludium" from *Ludus Tonalis*, mm. 1–10. ©
Schott and Co., Ltd., London, 1943; © Renewed. All rights
reserved. Used by permission of European American Music
Distributors Corporation, sole U.S. agent for Schott and Co., Ltd.

A lack of familiarity with Hindemith's harmonic and melodic language does not interfere with the perception of cadence in m. 10 of Example 1.4.

NOTE

1. The clear reduction of dissonance on the downbeat of the tenth measure
   produces the sensation of harmonic cadence.
2. The melodic goal of D is reached in the outer voices.
3. The continuation of the rhythmic activity prolongs the cadence.

In the following instances, structural phenomena are produced by
changes in various musical elements. The perception of structural division is
reinforced by such changes when associated with cadential phenomena.
Independent of cadence, they may be important cues for the perception of
structural division heard as the music unfolds rather than at a point of
repose.

Tonality.   An abrupt change *in key or mode* may be a structural phenomenon. This change may or may not be visible as a change in key
signature.

Example 1.5 Haydn: Divertimento in C major, Menuet and Trio, mm. 13–28

The change in mode from C major to C minor in m. 21 of Example 1.5 is evident both visually and aurally, and serves in this case as a strong structural phenomenon.

Example 1.6 Chopin: Prelude in B-flat major, Op. 28, No. 21, mm. 1–20

Highly chromatic though the first sixteen measures of Example 1.6 are, the music remains unmistakably in the key of B-flat. The dramatic change to G-flat major in m. 17 is a clearly perceived structural phenomenon.

NOTE

Unlike the change in Example 1.5, this change in tonality is accomplished without a change in key signature.

Tempo.   Changes in the *speed of the beat* may be structural phenomena. These changes may be approached gradually by accelerandi or ritardandi, or they may occur suddenly. The presence of gradual speeding up or slowing down may or may not signal a *structural* change in tempo.

Example 1.7   Ravel: *Le Tombeau de Couperin,* Rigaudon, mm. 25–45. ©
1918 Durand S.A. Editions Musicales. Editions Arima and
Durand S.A. Editions Musicales, Joint Publication. Used By
Permission Of The Publisher, Theodore Presser Company, Sole
Representative U.S.A. & Canada.

In Example 1.7, the change in tempo occurs abruptly in m. 37. The continuation of the eighth-note accompaniment figure heard in mm. 34 and 36 in the previous tempo makes the change in m. 37 more easily perceived as a structural phenomenon.

Example 1.8 Beethoven: Sonata in F minor, Op. 57, I, mm. 231–241

In Example 1.8, two changes in tempo produce evidence of a structural break at the double bar following m. 238. The first is preceded by a ritardando beginning in m. 235. The second occurs abruptly in m. 239.

NOTE

The *piu allegro* marking indicates a faster tempo than that which prevails in the rest of the movement. The *adagio* that precedes it enhances by comparison the perception of this structural phenomenon.

Meter.   An audible change in the *organization of subdivisions within beats, or of beats within measures,* may be a structural phenomenon. This change may be visible as a change in meter signature, or it may occur more subtly as a change in rhythmic organization.

Example 1.9   Brahms: Romance in F major, Op. 118, No. 5, mm. 13–21

The metrical change from 6/4 to 2/2 in m. 17 of Example 1.9 is obviously only one of a number of phenomena that produce a structural division at that point.

NOTE

With reference to the metrical organization, m. 16, which is in 3/2, serves as a transition between the compound duple in m. 15 and the simple duple in m. 17.

Example 1.10   Brahms: Intermezzo in E minor, Op. 119, No. 2, mm. 9–17

In m. 13 of Example 1.10, there is no change in meter signature. A structural phenomenon is created, however, by a clearly perceived change in metrical organization from 3/4 to 9/8.

Rhythm.   A *systematic change in prevailing note value,* without a change in tempo or meter, may be a structural phenomenon.

Example 1.11   Beethoven: Sonata in C major, Op. 53, I, mm. 27–46

Example 1.11 *(cont.)*

Several easily perceived changes in rhythmic content occur in Example 1.11. In m. 31, the prevailing sixteenth-note motion gives way to motion in eighth notes, and the density decreases again in m. 35.

NOTE

1. The contrast in prevailing rhythmic content that is established in m. 35 makes the change in density at that point the most convincing rhythmic structural phenomenon.

2. The absence of eighth- and sixteenth-note activity in m. 35 produces a per-

ceived change in meter from 4/4 to 2/2 that reinforces the importance of this point as a structural division.

3. A smaller structural division occurs with the introduction of the triplet figure in m. 42.

Dynamics. A change in *volume* can be an important indication of structural division. Like changes in tempo, changes in dynamics may be approached gradually—by crescendi or decrescendi—or they may occur abruptly. These changes may be visually indicated by the editor's markings, or they may be the result of changes in other related elements, such as density (discussed later).

Example 1.12 Chopin: Prelude in C minor, Op. 28, No. 20

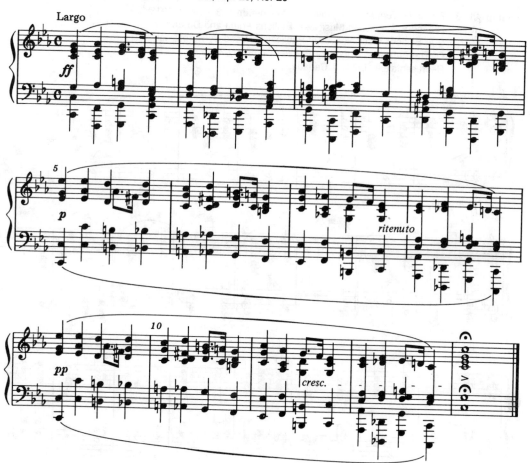

In Example 1.12, two changes in dynamics, indicated here by editor's markings in mm. 5 and 9, contribute to the perception of structural divisions.

NOTE

1. In both cases, perception of structural division is reinforced by a cadence on the fourth quarter note in the preceding measure.
2. Because the music is otherwise identical in mm. 5–8 and mm. 9–12, the importance of dynamic change alone as a structural phenomenon is made evident.
3. The perception of the subtle change in dynamics in m. 9 is enhanced by a change of tempo in mm. 7 and 8.

Example 1.13   Ravel: *Le Tombeau de Couperin,* Menuet, mm. 33–72. © 1918 Durand S.A. Editions Musicales. Editions Arima and Durand S.A. Editions Musicales, Joint Publication. Used By Permission Of The Publisher, Theodore Presser Company, Sole Representative U.S.A. & Canada.

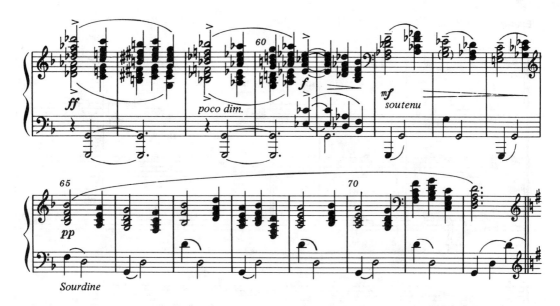

Changes in dynamics, approached gradually in Example 1.13, mark virtually all structural divisions in this short piece.

Density. A change in the *amount of musical space filled* may be associated with a break in the design.

Example 1.14 Palestrina: *Missa Veni sponsa Christi*, Kyrie, mm. 12–27

Example 1.14 *(cont.)*

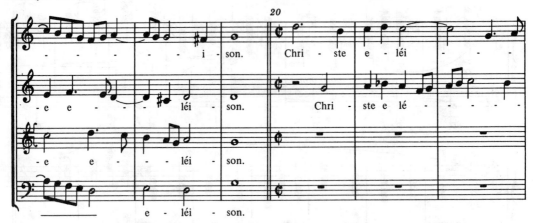

The absence of the two lower voices in mm. 20–24 of Example 1.14 creates a readily noticeable change in density from the fuller sound that precedes it. Occurring after the cadence in m. 19, this change contributes to the perception of a break in the structure.

NOTE

In mm. 25 and 27, less obvious changes in density, also preceded by cadences, produce structural divisions on a lower level.

Example 1.15 J. S. Bach: *W.T.C.,* Vol. II, Fugue 16 in G minor, mm. 59–68

In Example 1.15, the sudden reduction of voices in m. 67, preceded by a half-cadence, makes the structural division at this point easily heard.

Example 1.16 Bartók: *Mikrokosmos,* No. 149, mm. 13–20. © Copyright 1940 by Hawkes & Son (London) Ltd.; Renewed 1967. Reprinted by permission of Boosey & Hawkes, Inc.

Example 1.16 *(cont.)*

The sixteenth measure of Example 1.16 again illustrates that a change in density accompanies an important structural division. Dynamic change reinforces this phenomenon.

Timbre.   A change in *tone color,* that property of sound which allows the ear to distinguish between one instrument and another, or between one group of instruments and another, may easily be perceived as a structural phenomenon.

Example 1.17   Haydn: Symphony No. 100 in G major, I, mm. 24–43

Example 1.17 features very clear changes of timbre in mm. 32 and 39. Both changes are readily perceived as structural phenomena.

NOTE

In this case, both timbral changes are reinforced by changes in density.

Register. An abrupt change in the *range in which musical events occur* may be perceived as a structural phenomenon.

Example 1.18   Beethoven: Sonata in F minor, Op. 57, I, mm. 35–41

Example 1.18 (cont.)

In Example 1.18, the abrupt change in register in the right-hand part at the end of m. 39 is a structural phenomenon.

NOTE

The change in register in the left-hand part at the beginning of m. 39 serves as a preparation for the more obvious one at the end of the measure.

Example 1.19   Bartók: *Mikrokosmos*, No. 109, mm. 1–16. © Copyright 1940 by Hawkes & Son (London) Ltd.; Renewed 1967. Reprinted by permission of Boosey & Hawkes, Inc.

In the anacrusis to m. 13 of Example 1.19, a change in register is one of a number of phenomena that contribute to the perception of a structural division.

Texture.   A change in the *rhythmic and melodic relationships between voices* is often an easily perceived structural phenomenon.

Example 1.20   Gesualdo: "Beltà, poi che t'assenti," Madrigals Book VI, mm. 1–7. Used by permission of VEB Deutscher Verlag für Musik.

Example 1.20 *(cont.)*

The chordal texture, in which this madrigal (Example 1.20) begins, gives way to a contrapuntal texture in m. 5. That, combined with a change in density, creates a structural division.

Example 1.21   Beethoven: Sonata in E major, Op. 14, No. 1, I, mm. 38–55

The prevailing texture at the beginning of Example 1.21 is melody and accompaniment. In m. 46, however, a quasi-chordal texture is introduced, followed by a fully chordal texture in m. 50. Both points are perceived as structural divisions.

Motive.   The *return of a prominent melodic or rhythmic event* may signal a division in the design, and so may be considered a structural phenomenon. Such a return may be literal or somewhat altered. The perception of motivic return as a structural phenomenon, unlike those previously discussed, depends upon the listener's retention of formerly heard material over a longer time span.

Example 1.22   Mozart: Piano Sonata in D major, K. 284, III (Theme)

Example 1.22 *(cont.)*

The recognition of the return of the opening material in mm. 5 and 13 in Example 1.22 contributes to the perception of important structural divisions.

NOTE

1. While the structural divisions are recognizable through dynamic, textural, and cadential phenomena as well, motivic retention adds a critical dimension to the process of perception.
2. The division in m. 13 depends more heavily on motivic retention for perception because of the longer time span between motivic occurrences.

Example 1.23   C.P.E. Bach: Sonata III in F minor (1781), first movement, mm. 1–4, 31–38, 60–68

The first two measures of Example 1.23 illustrate the distinctive melodic and rhythmic event that opens this movement. In m. 35, there is a return of the same material in A-flat major, and in m. 65 an almost literal return in F minor. As in Example 1.22, the structural divisions at mm. 35 and 65 are made noticeable through other structural phenomena. There is no doubt, however, that the return of motivic material alone is an important phenomenon at these points.

Example 1.24   Schoenberg: Klavierstücke, Op. 33a (1929), mm. 1–11. Used
by permission of Belmont Music Publishers.

A comparison of mm. 1 and 10 in Example 1.24 illustrates the motivic structural phenomenon clearly. It is the recognition of the rhythmic and textual events of the opening measure, supported by a return to the original tempo, that contributes to the perception of structural division in m. 10.

NOTE

A comparison of the pitch content of the chords on the downbeats of mm. 1–2 and mm. 10–11 reveals a perceivable melodic and harmonic return in spite of the dissonance and the complexity of Schoenberg's harmonic language.

It should be clear that not all these phenomena are structurally significant in all music. In addition, it will become clear that the coincidence of more than one of these phenomena may be a clue for creating a hierarchy of breaking points in the design. Decisions regarding the relative importance of various points are made, therefore, with sensitivity to the musical context in mind.

EXERCISES

The exercises that follow are designed to provide experiences in the aural and visual identification of structural phenomena as they occur in complete musical contexts. In addition, decisions regarding the relative importance of structural divisions, and some observations about the nature of the structure, are required. These decisions and observations should be based on the information gathered by the identification of the structural phenomena.

The exercises may be done in class, or, where appropriate opportunities for hearing the music are provided, they may be done as independent assignments.

Study the analytical model, and apply the instructions for analysis to each of the exercises.

Analytical Model

1. With the score, listen to "An Important Event" by Schumann as many times as is necessary to become familiar with the music.

2. On the score, mark the conclusion of each cadence with a bracket (]). Inside the bracket, mark, where applicable, cadence types, using the following abbreviations: Authentic—A; Plagal—P; Half—H; Deceptive—D. (E.g., "A].")

3. While listening to the music, list the other structural phenomena on the score as shown, using the following abbreviations. (Make all preliminary markings in pencil.)

tonality:	ton
tempo:	tem
meter:	met
rhythm:	rhy
dynamics:	dyn
density:	den
timbre:	tim
register:	reg
texture:	tex
motive:	mot

4. When changes in tonality occur, ascertain the new tonality, and write it in parentheses next to the abbreviation "ton" on the score; e.g., "ton (A major)."

5. Mark the points of structural division on the score as shown, using an asterisk (*) to do so.

6. Based upon the number of structural phenomena that coincide in a given measure, beside each asterisk write "SD" to designate what you consider an important structural division; write "sd" for all others.

7. As a result of your analysis, make some brief observations about the organization of the music.

Analytical Model   Schumann: *Scenes from Childhood*, Op. 15, "An Important Event"

OBSERVATIONS

The piece is in three large sections. The third section is like the first section. The second section has no structural divisions within it; thus, it is more continuous than the first or the third sections. It is also in a different key from the outer sections. The second section represents a major *contrast* to the first and the third sections.

Most of the exercises are taken from Mary Wennerstrom's *Anthology of Musical Structure and Style* (Englewood Cliffs, N.J.: Prentice-Hall, 1983), Charles Burkhart's *Anthology for Musical Analysis,* 4th edition (New York: Holt, Rinehart, 1977), Ralph Turek's *Analytical Anthology of Music* (New York: Knopf, 1984), and Roger Kamien's *The Norton Scores,* 4th edition expanded (New York: W. W. Norton & Co., Inc., 1977). Other exercises from literature not found in these anthologies are included.

1. Schumann: *Carnaval,* Op. 9, No. 4, "Valse noble"
   (Wennerstrom, pp. 317–318)

2. Bartók: *Mikrokosmos,* No. 109, "From the Island of Bali"
   (Wennerstrom, pp. 479–480)

3. Schubert: *Six Moments Musical,* Op. 94, No. 6, mm. 1–77
   (Burkhart, pp. 334–335)

4. Schumann: *Album for the Young,* Op. 68, No. 8, "The Wild Rider"
   (Burkhart, pp. 340–341)

5. Haydn: String Quartet, Op. 9, No. 3, II
   (Turek, pp. 287–288)

6. Schumann: *Scenes from Childhood,* Op. 15, "By the Fireside"
   (Turek, p. 482)

7. Handel: *Messiah,* No. 2, "Comfort Ye"
   (Norton Scores I, pp. 140–142)

8. Mozart: *Eine kleine Nachtmusik,* III
   (Norton Scores I, pp. 493–494)

9. Schumann: *Album for the Young,* Op. 68, No. 11, "Sicilian"

10. Mozart: Sonata, K. 331, I, Tema

2
structural
units

INTRODUCTION

The analytical process set forth in Chapter 1 demonstrates that structural phenomena produce structural divisions in the design of complete pieces. Music, therefore, is initially perceived in structural units. This chapter explores the hierarchy of units within complete pieces of music and provides the beginning of a vocabulary with which relationships between units can be described.

Section

The term *section* may refer to a major structural unit perceived as the result of the coincidence of relatively large numbers of structural phenomena. However, the term may be used to define smaller structural units. Thus, a large section may be composed of a number of smaller ones.

For example, the analysis of Schumann's "An Important Event" on pages 28–29 showed three major sections separated by important structural divisions and by double bars. The first major section is itself composed of four smaller sections defined primarily by cadences.

Example 2.1 is also perceived in three major sections. In this case, the important structural divisions result principally from changes in tonality and texture.

Example 2.1   Chopin: Prelude in B-flat major, Op. 28, No. 21

Example 2.1 *(cont.)*

NOTE
1. The major sections are not separated by double bars.
2. The first major section consists of at least two shorter sections marked by cadential activity in mm. 7–8 and mm. 15–16.

Period

Much of the music studied previously has been perceived in large sections subdivided into smaller units, primarily by cadential structural phenomena. In such music, the description of relationships between these smaller units may become a useful analytical tool.

The *period,* a structural unit analogous to the sentence, is typically constructed of two or more smaller units called *phrases.* If the phrase is defined as the smallest structural unit that terminates with a cadence, the period may be understood as a logical grouping of phrases that gives an impression of closure.

Closure is perceived as the result of a hierarchy of cadential activity, the most decisive cadence occurring at the period's end. In all cases, the relatively inconclusive cadence at the end of the opening, or *antecedent,* phrase produces the necessity for completion, which is provided by the *consequent* phrase or phrases that follow. The identity of the period as a single structural unit depends on audible relationships between the various phenomena that characterize the phrases within it.

Examples 2.2–2.9 illustrate how cadence and phrase content interact to create structural units that are termed *periodic.*

Example 2.2   Schumann: *Album for the Young*, Op. 68, No. 8, "The Wild
Rider," mm. 1—8

"The Wild Rider" is made up of three periods, the first of which is exemplified in Example 2.2.

NOTE

1. The period consists of two phrases, the antecedent ending with a half-cadence in m. 4, and the consequent with a perfect authentic cadence in m. 8. The inconclusive cadence at the end of the first phrase, balanced as it is by the conclusive authentic cadence at the end of the second, is typical of simple period structure.

2. Because the musical content of the two phrases is essentially the same, this structural unit is described as a *parallel period*. (A glossary of terms will be found on page 47.)

3. Because the two phrases are of equal length, the period is described as *symmetrical*.

Example 2.3   Schubert: Waltz, Op. 9, No. 29, mm. 1—8

Example 2.3 *(cont.)*

   With the exception of the cadence structure, the period in Example 2.3 has the same characteristics as the one in Example 2.2.

   NOTE

1. Although the cadences that conclude the two phrases are similar, the perfect authentic cadence in m. 8 produces a stronger sense of closure than the imperfect one in m. 4.
2. In spite of a change of register at the beginning of the second phrase, the musical content of the two phrases is similar enough to describe the period as parallel.
3. The period consists of two four-measure phrases; thus, it is symmetrical.

Example 2.4   Mozart: Piano Sonata in B-flat major, K. 333, II, mm. 1–8

   This period (Example 2.4), which consists of two symmetrical phrases, is similar in tonal design to that in Example 2.2.

NOTE

1. Because the melodic content of the second phrase is substantially different from that of the first, the structural unit is considered to be a *contrasting period.*
2. The cadence that terminates the first phrase occurs on the second beat of the fourth measure. The second phrase, which begins on the downbeat of m. 5, is joined to the first by a melodic *link.*

Example 2.5 J. S. Bach: French Suite in E major, Gavotte, mm. 1–8

This parallel and symmetrical period (Example 2.5) is made up of two phrases, the first concluding with an imperfect authentic cadence in E major, and the second with a perfect authentic cadence in B major.

NOTE

1. Unlike Examples 2.2–2.5, the second phrase in this period contains a modulation to the dominant key, and thus the period is termed a *modulating period.* In spite of the modulation, the perfect authentic cadence in m. 8 provides the sense of closure typical of period structure.
2. The second phrase begins on the third beat of m. 4 and thus coincides with the cadence point of the first phrase. The simultaneous conclusion of one phrase with the opening of another is termed *elision.*

Example 2.6 Mozart: Sonata in G major, K. 283, I, mm. 1–10

The cadential structure of the period in Example 2.6 is like that in Example 2.3. Because the second phrase differs from the first both melodically and texturally, the period is contrasting.

NOTE

1. The second phrase is two measures longer than the first; therefore, the period is described as *asymmetrical*.
2. The harmonic activity in m. 7 and the length of the antecedent phrase produce the expectation of an authentic cadence on the downbeat of m. 8. Although the tonic harmony is present at that point, the melodic goal is not reached until the downbeat of m. 10, where the cadence occurs. Because mm. 8–9 serve to lengthen the second phrase by delaying the cadence, the asymmetrical structure is the result of *cadential extension*.

Example 2.7 Chopin: Mazurka in B-flat major, Op. 7, No. 1, mm. 1–24

Example 2.7 is the first major section of the mazurka. It consists of a single period of twelve measures, repeated.

NOTE

1. Unlike all previous examples, this period contains *three* symmetrical phrases, the first ending in a plagal cadence in m. 4, the second in an imperfect authentic cadence in m. 8, and the third in a perfect authentic cadence in m. 12.

2. In this case, both the second and the third phrases are perceived as consequent to the first. Because the melodic content of these phrases differs from the first, the period is contrasting.

3. The melodic figure that terminates the first phrase becomes the primary melodic idea for the second and, thus, might be mistaken for the beginning of

that phrase. It should be emphasized, however, that the phrases in this period are clearly delineated by the cadences.

Example 2.8   Chopin: Mazurka in A minor, Op. 7, No. 2, mm. 1–16

Example 2.8 is a four-phrase symmetrical period whose cadence structure differs from those previously discussed.

NOTE

1. The metrically strong half-cadence in m. 8 divides the period into two parts that create the antecedent and consequent structure.
2. The relatively weak imperfect authentic cadence in m. 4 and the deceptive cadence in m. 12 divide each part into pairs of contrasting phrases; however, since the melodic content of the first two phrases is similar to that of the second two, the period is considered parallel.
3. In this case, the antecedent-consequent phrase structure of the simple two-phrase parallel period has been expanded to two *pairs* of phrases. This structure is termed a *double period.*

Example 2.9   Bartók: *Mikrokosmos,* No. 109, mm. 1–11. © Copyright 1940 by
Hawkes & Son (London) Ltd.; Renewed 1967. Reprinted by
permission of Boosey & Hawkes, Inc.

Although the tonal organization of Example 2.9 is different from
those previously studied, the melodic structure is typical of a simple parallel period.

NOTE

1. The periodic antecedent-consequent structure is preserved by the rhythmic
   strength of the cadence in m. 11 compared with that in m. 4.
2. The period is asymmetrical as a result of extension in the second phrase.

Phrase Groups

Periodic structure describes only one way in which phrases are combined to make larger sections of music. In many sections typical of extended pieces of music, the conclusive nature of period structure is not
appropriate for the design. Sections in which phrases are linked by a series
of cadences of an inconclusive nature are often termed *phrase groups.* Terminology that addresses the relations between melodic and rhythmic content (parallel/contrasting) and phrase length (symmetrical/asymmetrical)
may be used in describing phrase groups, but the antecedent-consequent
cadential structure is absent.

Example 2.10 Schumann: *Carnaval*, Op. 9, No. 4, mm. 1–32

Whereas the first eight measures of Example 2.10 are clearly periodic, mm. 9–24 represent a discrete section consisting· of four four-measure phrases, none of which ends with a conclusive cadence. This section is termed a *phrase group*. The measures that follow show a return to the period structure with which the piece opens.

Example 2.11   Haydn: Sonata in E major, Hob. XVI/13, II, Menuetto

Example 2.11 *(cont.)*

The opening section of Example 2.11 consists of two four-measure phrases. Because the second phrase ends with a half-cadence in E major, the structure is not periodic; it is, therefore, a phrase group.

NOTE

1. Measures 15–24 represent a varied repetition of the opening section. In this case, the structure is periodic.
2. Comparison of mm. 19–24 with mm. 5–9 reveals that the symmetry of the original phrase group is destroyed by the insertion of mm. 21–22, so perceived because the remaining measures clearly parallel the content of the second phrase. Such an insertion is called an *interpolation*.

Example 2.12 Beethoven: Sonata in E-flat major, Op. 81a, I, mm. 1–17

attacca subito l' Allegro

In Example 2.12, the Adagio is a phrase group consisting of three four-measure phrases, the last of which is extended to m. 17, where the Allegro begins. The tonal instability of the section contributes to the inconclusive nature of all the cadences.

Other Structural Units

Virtually any structural unit that concludes with a cadence may be considered a phrase. Some structural units, however, because of the nature of their melodic or harmonic content, may not be described appropriately with terminology generally associated with periods or phrase groups. The term *section* may be applied to such units, or to a collection of them related by content.

Example 2.13   Chopin: Prelude in B-flat major, Op. 28, No. 21, mm. 33–58

Example 2.13 (cont.)

Measures 33–45 of Example 2.13 consist of two short sections that decorate and extend the dominant harmony in B-flat major. The sections are most noticeably separated by changes in structural phenomena. The second section, mm. 39–45, concludes with a cadence on tonic harmony. Because the harmonic content of these two sections is limited to an elaboration of dominant harmony, the entire unit is more appropriately described as a *cadential section* than as a phrase.

Likewise, the section from m. 45 to the end of the example contains nothing more than melodic fragments whose underlying harmonic content reiterates an authentic cadential motion that is plainly stated in the last two measures. Such a unit may be termed a *closing section* rather than a group of very short phrases consisting of two or three chords.

GLOSSARY

Asymmetrical: describes a period in which the phrases differ in length.

Cadential extension: the prolongation or delay of the cadence by the addition of material beyond the point at which the cadence is expected.

Contrasting: describes a period in which the musical content of the phrases differs.

Double period: a periodic structure in which the antecedent-consequent relationship is fulfilled by *pairs* of phrases.

Elision: the connection of two phrases in such a way that the cadential point of the first coincides with the beginning of the second.

Interpolation: the lengthening of the repetition of a phrase by the insertion of material not heard in the original phrase.

Link: material that appears between the end of one phrase and the beginning of the next but that belongs to neither.

Modulating: describes a period in which modulation occurs in the consequent phrase(s).

Parallel: describes a period in which the musical content of the phrases is the same.

Symmetrical: describes a period in which the phrases are the same length.

EXERCISES

Periodic Structures

Study the analytical model, and apply the instructions for analysis to each of the exercises.

1. Listen several times to the music provided.

2. On the score, mark the conclusion of each cadence with a bracket, and indicate its type.

3. Describe the organization of the period. The following points should be addressed where applicable:

  a. Phrase structure—number of phrases, double period construction, links, elisions.

  b. Modulation—key at end of period.

  c. Symmetry—extension, interpolation.

  d. Content—parallel/contrasting.

Analytical Model   Schumann: *Album for the Young,* Op. 68, No. 28, "Remembrance," mm. 1–10

  a. The period consists of two phrases.

  b. The second phrase modulates to E major.

  c. The period is asymmetrical because the second phrase is extended by a deceptive resolution of V^7 in E major in m. 8.

  d. This is a parallel period.

1. J. S. Bach: French Suite in E major, Sarabande, mm. 1–8 (Wennerstrom, p. 119)

2. Mozart: *Don Giovanni,* "Mi tradì quell'alma ingrata," mm. 37–51 (Wennerstrom, p. 200)

3. Beethoven: Sonata in E major, Op. 14, No. 1, II, mm. 1–16, 33–51
   (Wennerstrom, pp. 233–234)

4. Schubert: Waltz, Op. 9, No. 29, mm. 17–24
   (Wennerstrom, p. 285)

5. Schubert: Waltz in A-flat major, Op. 9, No. 2, mm. 1–8
   (Burkhart, p. 333)

6. J. S. Bach(?): *Little Notebook of Anna Magdalena Bach,* "March," mm. 1–9
   (Burkhart, p. 81)

7. Mozart: Sonata in B-flat major, K. 333, I, mm. 23–38
   (Burkhart, p. 207)

8. Beethoven: Sonata in C minor, Op. 13, III, mm. 1–17
   (Burkhart, p. 275)

9. Mozart: Sonata in F major, K. 332, I, mm. 41–56
   (Turek, p. 319)

10. Mozart: *The Abduction from the Seraglio,* Act II, No. 8, mm. 9–18
    (Turek, p. 334)

11. Clementi: Sonatina, Op. 36, No. 3, I, mm. 1–12
    (Turek, p. 368)

12. Beethoven: Sonata in C major, Op. 53, I, mm. 35–42
    (Turek, p. 381)

13. Gluck: *Orfeo ed Euridice,* "Che farò senza Euridice," mm. 7–16
    (Norton Scores I, p. 309)

14. Beethoven: String Quartet, Op. 18, No. 1, I, mm. 1–20
    (Norton Scores I, p. 561)

15. Beethoven: Sonata in C minor, Op. 13, II, mm. 1–16
    (Norton Scores I, p. 580)

16. Schumann: *Fantasiestücke,* "Aufschwung," mm. 1–16
    (Norton Scores II, p. 217)

17. Mozart: Sonata in D major, K. 284, II, mm. 1–16

18. Beethoven: Sonata in A-flat major, Op. 26, I, mm. 1–16

19. Schumann: *Album for the Young,* Op. 68, No. 13, "May, Lovely May . . ." mm. 1–10

20. Chopin: Mazurka in A minor, Op. 59, No. 1, mm. 1–12

Complete Pieces

Analyze the following pieces in two stages:

First, use the analytical procedures from Chapter 1 to establish the large and small subdivisions in the structure.

Second, try to determine the nature of the internal structure of each of the major sections. Ask yourself whether a section is periodic, whether it is a phrase group, or whether it fits either designation.

Report the results of your analysis as you did in the preceding exercises.

1. Haydn: Divertimento in C major, Hob. XVI/1, Minuet and Trio
   (Wennerstrom, pp. 176–177)

2. Schubert: Waltz, Op. 9, No. 14
   (Wennerstrom, pp. 284–285)

3. Schumann: *Scenes from Childhood*, No. 13, "The Poet Speaks"
   (Wennerstrom, pp. 313–314)

4. J. S. Bach(?): *Little Notebook of Anna Magdalena Bach*, Minuet
   (Burkhart, pp. 82–83)

5. Schumann: *Album for the Young*, No. 17, "Little Morning Wanderer"
   (Burkhart, pp. 343–344)

6. Chopin: Mazurka in A minor, Op. posth. 67, No. 4
   (Burkhart, p. 366)

7. J. S. Bach: French Suite in E major, Menuet
   (Turek, p. 206)

8. Schumann: *Scenes from Childhood*, No. 8, "By the Fireside"
   (Turek, p. 482)

9. Chopin: Mazurka in E minor, Op. 17, No. 2
   (Turek, pp. 501–502)

10. Beethoven: Eleven Bagatelles, Op. 119, No. 9

11. J. S. Bach: French Suite in B minor, Menuet II

12. Mendelssohn: *Songs without Words*, Op. 30, No. 3

3

structural
functions

INTRODUCTION

Just as the parts of a book have specific purposes in the unfolding of the plot, similarly, structural units play functional roles in the organization of a piece of music. These units possess *internal* attributes that help to define their purpose in the music's construction. The perception of *structural function* through sensitivity to those attributes is an essential analytical tool in understanding the organizational principle of an entire piece.

The four basic structural functions defined in this chapter are termed *expository, transitional, developmental,* and *terminative.* The attributes that mark these functions are closely related to the phenomena described in Chapter 1 and to the interaction of structural units described in Chapter 2. It must be emphasized that the attributes that characterize each function frequently overlap with the attributes of the other functions, as do functions within sections of music. Nevertheless, sensitivity to these functional attributes is crucial in understanding the principles that govern musical composition.

Expository Function

The purpose of *expository* units is, as the word suggests, to *expose* musical materials that are important in the context of the complete structure's organization. They are analogous to those declarative passages in literary works that reveal primary topics or themes. Expository units, therefore, are typically characterized by clear phrase structure that is often periodic. In tonal music, harmonic activity that serves to establish a prevailing tonality reinforces the perception of expository function.

Example 3.1 illustrates how phrase structure and tonal organization interact with other attributes to create the perception of expository function.

Example 3.1   Haydn: Sonata in E minor, Hob. XVI/34, III, mm. 19–40

The first eight measures of Example 3.1 represent a modulating period. Following a less clearly defined structural unit of six measures, the example concludes with a period, the content of which is closely related to the first one.

NOTE

1. The first four measures of the example clearly exhibit the tonal stability and phrase structure associated with expository function.

2. Although the period is completed in mm. 23–26, the tonal attributes of expository function are no longer present as a result of the modulation to the dominant. The entire period, however, may be perceived as partially expository because of the clarity of the phrase structure.

3. In spite of the relatively stable tonal activity in mm. 27–32, the absence of a clearly defined phrase structure weakens the perception of this passage as expository.

4. In mm. 33–40, there is no modulation, and thus the period is entirely expository.

Transitional Function

Transitional sections often serve a connecting function between sections of relative repose in the musical context. Transitional passages, therefore, may possess attributes that support the perception of *movement*, such as unpredictable or fragmentary structural units, rhythmic agitation, dynamic contrasts, and frequent changes in other structural phenomena. In tonal music, they are characterized by harmonic activity that serves to dissolve the previously established key and to establish a new one.

Example 3.2   Beethoven: Sonata in G major, Op. 14, No. 2, i, mm. 1–33

Example 3.2 *(cont.)*

Measures 9–25 of Example 3.2 exhibit several of the attributes characteristic of transitional function. Most significant, the music modulates from G major to the dominant of D. The perception of movement is enhanced by continuously increasing rhythmic activity, by fragmented melodic units, and by frequent changes in dynamics.

NOTE

1. A gradual change in register is achieved by the stepwise ascent of the bass from m. 9 to m. 19.
2. The connecting role, typical of transitional units, is easily perceived because the passages that precede and follow this section clearly demonstrate expository function.

Developmental Function

Developmental sections are analogous to literary passages whose purpose is to amplify or to discuss ideas previously introduced. In musical contexts, then, the primary attribute of developmental passages is the presentation of motivic material heard previously in changed, or *varied*, form. In addition, such units are often tonally unstable and thus share some of the attributes associated with transitional function.

Example 3.3 Beethoven: Sonata in C major, Op. 2, No. 3, III, mm. 1–47

Example 3.3 *(cont.)*

Example 3.3 begins with a sixteen-measure modulating period, based primarily upon an eighth-note anacrusis figure followed by a descending scale pattern. Measures 17–28 clearly demonstrate developmental function. The motivic material of the first two measures is fragmented and altered intervallically. In addition, the section is tonally unstable, suggesting the keys of C minor, B-flat minor, and A-flat major before reaching a half-cadence in C minor. Throughout this section, no clear phrase structure prevails.

NOTE

1. Although the first phrase of the example is primarily expository in function because of its phrase structure and its stable tonality, the use of the opening motivic material in a contrapuntal texture within the unit produces the per-

ception of developmental function as well. Similarly, the second phrase (primarily transitional in tonal function) may be considered developmental in its motivic character.

2. Although mm. 29–39 are tonally static, the perception of developmental function continues through further motivic fragmentation, reinforced by sudden changes of register, texture, and dynamics.

3. The example ends with an eight-measure expository phrase, similar in content to the first one.

Terminative Function

As the term implies, the function of terminative passages is to bring sections or complete works to a close. The primary attribute of terminative sections is tonal activity that confirms and reinforces an established key. Continuous cadential activity and static tonality, then, typically mark such sections. Terminative passages may exhibit the clear phrase structure of expository units, or they may be more fragmentary in nature. Further, such units may involve the variation of previously exposed motivic material and thus may be partially developmental in function.

Example 3.4   Beethoven(?): Sonatina in G major, I

Example 3.4 *(cont.)*

Measures 25–34 of Example 3.4 represent a simple period followed by the reiteration of a G major triad. The alternation of dominant and tonic harmonies throughout the unit is typical of terminative function. Furthermore, the melody, which consists almost exclusively of members of the tonic triad, reinforces the static tonal quality of the section.

EXERCISES

The exercises in Chapter 1 involved the sectional analysis of a number of pieces of music by the identification of structural phenomena. In Chapter 2, emphasis was placed upon applying the appropriate terminology to the structural units that were identified.

Return to the following exercises in the two previous chapters, and determine the *structural functions* of both small and large sections.

Chapter 1: Exercises 1, 4, 5, 6, 8, 10.
Chapter 2: Exercises (Complete Pieces) 1, 5, 7, 9, 10.

4

the binary principle

INTRODUCTION

The binary principle is embodied at a low structural level in the two-phrase period in which the antecedent and the consequent phrases are typically interdependent. Thus, pieces of music divided into two main parts, the second of which is perceived as an outgrowth of the first, exemplify the principle. The parts are commonly labeled A and B. The binary principle has been employed in composition for several hundred years; an early example follows (Example 4.1).

Example 4.1 Walther von der Vogelweide (d. 1230): "Nu al'erst." From *Historical Anthology of Music,* Vol. I. Copyright © 1946, 1949 by the President and Fellows of Harvard College; renewed 1974 by Alice D. Humez and Willi Apel. Reprinted by permission of Harvard University Press.

1. Nu al - êrst le - be ich mir wer - de   Sit min sün - dic ou - ge siht
2. Hie daz land und auch die er - de   Den man vil der e - ren giht.

61

Example 4.1 *(cont.)*

3. Mirst ge - schehen des ich je - bat: Ich bin kom - men

an die stat Da got men - nisch - li - chen trat.

The most obvious evidence of a two-part division in this short piece in modern transcription is visual—the double bar at the end of the fourth measure. The logic of this division is emphasized by a melodic cadence on d in m. 4 and by a rhythmic change in m. 5. The change in rhythm accompanies the return of the opening motive at the interval of a perfect fifth higher. The song, then, is perceived as two clearly related structural units that, lacking the clear phrase structure associated with period, are best described as sections. The musical material in both sections is largely expository.

Example 4.2, written approximately 700 years after Vogelweide's song, is obviously much more complex, but nonetheless demonstrates the binary principle clearly.

Example 4.2   Krenek: 12 Short Piano Pieces, Op. 83, No. 2, "Peaceful Mood." Used by permission of G. Schirmer, Inc.

This movement, based upon eight iterations of a twelve-note row, is largely developmental in function. Although there is no double bar, the piece is divided into two parts by a single cadence in m. 5. The first beat of the sixth measure is particularly significant in emphasizing the binary division because, apart from the first beat of the piece, nowhere else is the absence of sound encountered. In addition, the dynamic marking of *pianissimo,* reserved for the cadences in the fifth and the final measures, reinforces the perception of repose.

The binary examples just cited are merely two of a large number that could have been chosen. Neither of them, as it happens, is really representative of the mainstream of musical activity in its respective century.In the seventeenth and early eighteenth centuries, however, increasing standardization of tonal movement and motivic treatment led to a type of design that gave birth to a host of compositions in which the binary principle was most effectively expressed. From these works gradually evolved the sonata-allegro structure (discussed in Chapter 8), an expanded and more flexible expression of the binary principle.

Elements of the Binary Principle

The binary principle, as it applies to simple binary, rounded binary, and sonata-allegro forms, is expressed above all else in terms of tonal movement. The first part of the structure (Part A) typically involves the motion from the tonic to an authentic cadence in a related key (or, less frequently, to a half-cadence in the original key). The role of the second part of the structure (Part B) is to return to and reestablish the tonic before the final cadence. Occasionally, binary movements are found in which Part A closes with an authentic cadence in the tonic key. In these movements, the interdependence of the two parts, on which the binary principle depends, rests primarily on motivic relationships.

The following diagram represents skeletal tonal movements typical of structures in major and minor keys.

Major Keys: I———V || V———I

Minor Keys: i———III || III———i
                     or
                     i———v || V———i

With respect to structural units and structural function, the role of the two parts is less clearly defined. This statement, however, may safely be made: The binary principle embodies (1) two major sections, which may or may not be subdivided into smaller ones, and (2) the process of movement away from, and back to, the tonic. Hence, each section demonstrates, in the broadest sense, transitional function.

It must be emphasized that simple binary, rounded binary, and sonata-allegro forms represent different expressions of the binary principle. It will be seen that the differences between them are matters of internal design. In each case, however, the *principle* is not violated.

Simple Binary Form

Simple binary, a form that dominated the instrumental dance suites of the Baroque era, typically involves the unfolding of a single musical idea in two main parts. The parts are separated by a double bar with repeat signs, and so are easy to identify visually. Usually each part is either a single, indivisible section or a phrase group. Periodic structure is rare. If it occurs, however, it is more likely to do so in Part A. The cadence structure at the end of each part matches the skeletal diagram on this page. The material in Part A is often expository and transitional in function, and sometimes developmental as well. Part B tends to be longer and less stable tonally than Part A. Developmental function, therefore, is commonly encountered after the double bar, followed by a closing section of expository and terminative function in the tonic.

NOTE

In simple binary form, the melodic/thematic material that was originally stated in the tonic in Part A is *not literally restated* in Part B.

Example 4.3 is typical of a simple binary form of the Baroque period.

Example 4.3   Blow: Courante

Part A consists of a single section that continues without pause to an authentic cadence in the dominant in m. 14. Functionally, it is expository, transitional, and developmental. Until the tonic is reestablished in m. 30, Part B is developmental in function. The last four measures are perceived, as a result of a repeated rhythmic pattern and clear harmonic motion in the tonic, as serving a terminative function.

NOTE

1. The material that first appeared in the tonic is never restated in that key.
2. The organization of the music does not lend itself well to phrase and period terminology.
3. Of the eleven structural phenomena identified in Chapter 1, cadence and motive alone play a significant role in the perception of the piece's sub-divisions.
4. Part B is five measures longer than Part A.

Example 4.4   J. S. Bach: French Suite in B minor, Minuet I

The basic tonal organization of Example 4.4 is typical of binary movements written in a minor key. The first sixteen measures constitute a modulating period of two eight-measure phrases. The first phrase is expository; the second is both expository and transitional. The symmetrical
periodic structure of Part A is not employed in Part B. Measures 17–24
represent a section with expository (the original melody is now stated in the
lower voice in D major), developmental (in the upper voice there is a
countermelodic line), and transitional (a modulation to F-sharp minor begins in m. 21) functions. The measures that follow give no sense of being
consequent. Measures 25–30 serve as a transition back to the tonic. Measures 31–36, now firmly in B minor, are expository and, to some degree,
terminative.

NOTE

1. The original melodic/thematic material is not restated in the tonic key after
    the double bar.
2. There is a change in texture after the double bar. This structural phe-
    nomenon is effectively used not only to reinforce a structural division but also
    to signal a change both in structural function and in unit organization of the
    movement.
3. Part B is four measures longer than Part A.

The Binary Principle in Simple Binary Form

The binary principle in simple binary form is expressed most clearly through tonality. The organization of the structural units that make up Parts A and B varies from movement to movement. Some movements exhibit a clearly defined phrase structure; some do not. Thus, with reference to structural function, it can be stated only that in Part A expository material is followed by transitional (and sometimes developmental) material, and that in Part B developmental material is followed by expository (and sometimes terminative) material. The principle is exemplified in the following diagram:

```
Part A                              Part B

I -----------------------------V || V-----------------------------------------I
i -----------------------------III || III -------------------------------------i
i -----------------------------v || V-----------------------------------------i

Phrase Group                        Phrase Group
Single Section                      Single Section
Period

Expository ---- Transitional        Developmental -------- Expository
            (Developmental)                          (Terminative)
```

EXERCISES

Study the analytical model, and apply the instructions for analysis to each of the pieces.

1. Listen several times to the music provided.

2. On the score, mark the conclusion of each cadence with a bracket, and indicate its type and the key at that point. Use uppercase letters for major keys; use lowercase letters for minor keys.

3. List changes (if any) in tonality, tempo, meter, and so on that create structural phenomena.

4. Describe the organization of Parts A and B. First, answer the following questions individually in note form. Then, write a short paragraph that demonstrates your understanding of the binary principle as it applies to this piece of music.

    a. What are the important structural phenomena?

    b. What is the key and cadence scheme?

    c. How are the structural units organized (periods, phrase groups, sections, etc.)?

    d. What is the structural function of each unit?

Analytical Model Bach: French Suite in D minor, Sarabande

Part A

Measures 1–8: Cadence marks the end of the section. Tonic in D minor to half-cadence in same key. One continuous phrase. Expository.

Part B

Measures 9–16: Marked by cadential phenomena; also change in texture. Dominant in D major to authentic cadence in G minor. Single phrase. Developmental and transitional function.

Measures 17–24: Marked by changes in texture and tonality. Dominant in F major to authentic cadence in D minor. Single phrase. Developmental and expository function.

The double bar divides the Sarabande into two major sections. Part A consists of a single phrase that terminates in a half-cadence in the tonic key. Its role is expository. Part B may be divided into two phrases. The first concludes with an authentic cadence in G minor in m. 16, the second with an authentic cadence in D minor (Picardy third) at the end of the piece. A change in texture reinforces the perception of the beginning of Part B, and a similar textural change as well as an implied change in tonality (a shift to F major) helps to identify the last phrase. Much of Part B is developmental, although the rather direct movement from the dominant of D minor to G minor suggests a transitional function as well. Measure 20 signals the return of the tonic key, and the last five measures, being tonally stable, play an expository role.

1. J. S. Bach: Goldberg Variations, Aria
   (Wennerstrom, pp. 111–112)

2. J. S. Bach: French Suite in E major, Gavotte
   (Wennerstrom, p. 120)

3. J. S. Bach: English Suite in G minor, Gavotte I
   (Burkhart, pp. 110–111)

4. J. S. Bach: Suite in G major for Violoncello, Minuets I and II
   (Burkhart, pp. 113–114)

5. J. S. Bach: French Suite in E major, Polonaise
   (Turek, p. 205)

6. Handel: Suite in D minor for Harpsichord, Allemande
   (Turek, p. 247)

7. J. S. Bach: Suite No. 3 in D major, Air
   (Norton Scores I, pp. 226–227)

8. J. S. Bach: French Suite in G major, Allemande, Sarabande

9. J. S. Bach: French Suite in C minor, Courante, Gigue

Rounded Binary Form

The observations that introduced the section on simple binary apply equally well to rounded binary, particularly with reference to tonality. There is one exception, however. In a rounded binary structure, *the original melodic/thematic material returns in Part B in the tonic key.* The word *rounded,* therefore, refers to the rounding out of the structure as a result of such a return.

Although an occasional movement in rounded binary form may be found in Baroque dance suite movements, the structure was more systematically employed throughout the Classic period. As a result, there is a tendency for the organization of the phrases to be more symmetrical, particularly in Part A where periodic structure is commonly encountered.

Example 4.5 clearly illustrates a straightforward rounded binary structure.

Example 4.5   Haydn: Sonata in D major, Hob. XVI/14, II, Menuetto

Example 4.5 *(cont.)*

Part A is a contrasting, modulating period, consisting of two four-measure phrases. The first is expository in function; the second is transitional. Part B is made up of a six-measure section in which a modulation from A major to D major occurs, followed by a two-phrase period whose antecedent phrase is identical to the first phrase of the piece and whose consequent phrase is an exact transposition of the second. The function of mm. 9–14 is transitional; that of mm. 15–22 is expository and terminative.

NOTE

1. The movement is in *rounded* binary form because the original material is repeated *in the tonic* in Part B.
2. Measures 9 and 14 are perceived as initiating sections largely as a result of the strong cadences that precede them. Changes in register also contribute to the perception of these points as being structurally significant.
3. Part B is six measures longer than Part A.

Example 4.6 is interesting because it shows the application of the binary principle in an expanded rounded binary form.

Example 4.6   Beethoven: Sonata in F major, Op. 10, No. 2, II, mm. 1–38

Measures 1–8 represent a period that begins in F minor and terminates with an authentic cadence in A-flat major. Functionally, therefore, the period is perceived as being both expository and transitional. Measures 9–16 serve both a transitional and a developmental function. The music passes from A-flat major through B-flat minor to the dominant of F minor. The fermata lends weight to the half-cadence. The remaining twenty-two measures in F minor are closely related to the material at the beginning of the movement. A period spans mm. 17–30. The antecedent phrase, compared with mm. 1–4, is extended by two measures; the consequent, compared with mm. 5–8, by four. The function is mainly expository, but the phrase extensions suggest developmental function as well. Measures 31–38, in which an elaborated authentic cadence occurs twice, obviously serve a terminative function.

NOTE

1. The rounding-out process begins in m. 17 in the tonic.
2. Each of the important structural divisions is articulated by one or more structural phenomena, changes in texture and dynamics being particularly significant.
3. Part B is almost four times as long as Part A.

The Binary Principle in Rounded Binary Form

As in simple binary, the binary principle in rounded binary form is most clearly expressed through tonality. The return of the tonic key, however, is associated with a return of the original melodic/thematic material, and so a motivic principle is also involved. Motive as a structural phenomenon plays a role in the perception of the design that it did not play in simple binary movements. The binary principle is expanded to some extent, too, to the unit organization of the two parts. Part A is commonly a modulating period; Part B, following a phrase or a group of phrases, often terminates with a period whose content is based upon the first one. Functionally, then, Part A is expository and transitional; Part B is developmental (transitional) and expository. The principle is exemplified in the following diagram. It should be compared with the diagram that exemplifies the principle in simple binary form (see page 68).

Part A		Part B		
I --------------------V ||	V --------------------------------V–I --------------------I			
i -----------------III ||	III ----------------------------------V–i ---------------------i			
i --------------------v ||	V --------------------------------V–i ---------------------i			
Theme				Theme
Period		Phrase Group		Period
Expository -----		Developmental ------------------		Expository
-------Transitional		(Transitional)		(Terminative)

EXERCISES

Apply the instructions for analysis to each of the following pieces. (You may wish to review the analytical model on page 69 before you begin.)

1. Listen several times to the music provided.

2. On the score, mark the conclusion of each cadence with a bracket, and indicate its type and the key at that point. Use uppercase letters for major keys, lowercase for minor keys.

3. List changes (if any) in tonality, tempo, meter, and so on that create structural phenomena.

4. Describe the organization of Parts A and B. First, answer the following questions individually in note form. Then, write a short paragraph that demonstrates your understanding of the binary principle as it applies to this piece of music.

> **a.** What are the important structural phenomena?
>
> **b.** What is the key and cadence scheme?
>
> **c.** How are the structural units organized?
>
> **d.** What is the structural function of each unit?
>
> **e.** Where does the rounding out begin?

1. Haydn: Divertimento in C major, Menuet, Trio
(Wennerstrom, pp. 176–177)

2. Beethoven: Sonata in E major, Op. 14, No. 1, Allegretto, mm. 1–61
(Wennerstrom, pp. 235–236)

3. Beethoven: Sonata in F minor, Op. 2, No. 1, Menuetto, Trio
(Burkhart, pp. 264–265)

4. Beethoven: Sonata in D major, Op. 28, Scherzo
(Burkhart, pp. 294–295)

5. Mozart: String Quintet in G minor, K. 516, II, Minuetto, Trio
(Turek, pp. 365–367)

6. Mozart: *Eine kleine Nachtmusik,* III, Menuetto
(Norton Scores I, p. 493)

7. Haydn: Sonata in D major, Hob. XVI/27, II, Menuet, Trio

8. Mozart: Sonata in E-flat major, K. 282, II, Menuetto I

9. Mozart: Sonata in A major, K. 331, II, Menuetto

10. Schumann: *Scenes from Childhood,* Op. 15, No. 7, "Reveries"

5

the ternary principle

INTRODUCTION

The ternary principle is fundamentally one of *statement, contrast,* and *restatement.* Thus, it is embodied in pieces of music that are divided into three main parts, the second of which is perceived as differing substantially from similar first and third parts. The parts of standard ternary movements are labeled A-B-A.

Like the binary principle, the ternary principle may be perceived in music spanning several hundred years. Two early examples follow.

Example 5.1 "C'est la fin" (Virelai), twelfth century (?). From *Historical Anthology of Music,* Vol. I. Copyright © 1946, 1949 by the President and Fellows of Harvard College; renewed 1974 by Alice D. Humez and Willi Apel. Reprinted by permission of Harvard University Press.

1. C'est la fin, koi que nus di - e, j'a - me - rais.

2. C'est la jus en mis les prês, 3. C'est la fin, je veul a -

The first phrase of Example 5.1, reaching a cadence on D in m. 6, represents *statement* in this small ternary design.

Contrast, perceived both in the length of the phrases and in a tonal emphasis on A, is provided by the music that accompanies the second and third lines of the poetry.

Restatement is heard as the first phrase (repeated) is used for the fourth and fifth lines of poetry.

The ternary design of Example 5.2 may be perceived both aurally and visually.

Example 5.2   Juan Encina (d.ca. 1530): "Pues que jamás" (Villancico). From *Historical Anthology of Music,* Vol. I. Copyright © 1946, 1949 by the President and Fellows of Harvard College; renewed 1974 by Alice D. Humez and Willi Apel. Reprinted by permission of Harvard University Press.

Example 5.2 *(cont.)*

Da capo al Fine

Part A (to the double bar) is perceived as an asymmetrical two-phrase period. The first cadence is elided on the downbeat of m. 9; the second is authentic in F in m. 15.

Part B, consisting of two shorter phrases, is repeated for the second and third lines of poetry. Contrast is provided, as in Example 5.1, by tonal emphasis and by phrase length. The first phrase ends with an authentic cadence in F in m. 19, the second with a half-cadence in m. 22.

The *da capo* visually demonstrates the restatement of the first period.

NOTE

In these examples, contrast is perceived primarily in the manipulation of the limited tonal resources of the period. In each case, however, the B section is perceived as tonally *open,* an attribute observed in analogous sections as the ternary principle evolves.

Simple Ternary Form

The essentials of the ternary principle are illustrated clearly in Examples 5.1 and 5.2. As in the case of the binary principle, the seventeenth and eighteenth centuries produced formal procedures that further defined the principle in tonal, functional, and motivic terms. The Baroque *da capo aria* that follows is an example of such a procedure (Example 5.3).

Example 5.3   Handel: *Julius Caesar,* Piangerò la sorte mia

Example 5.3 *(cont.)*

Example 5.3 *(cont.)*

The three basic divisions are easily perceived as the results of the coincidence of a number of very clear structural phenomena in m. 48 and the repeat of m. 1. In m. 48, following a strong authentic cadence in E major, changes in tonality, tempo, meter, texture, and rhythmic content are clearly evident. Similarly, after an authentic cadence in G-sharp minor in m. 69, the repeat of m. 1 produces changes in tonality, meter, tempo, and rhythm.

The strong contrast provided by Part B in Example 5.3 emphasizes a fundamental functional principle of ternary organization. Developmental function, which in part defines the relationship between Parts A and B in mature binary structures, is absent from typical ternary structures.

The cadences with which the large sections of this example close reveal a tonal principle that further defines relationships among the sections. Part A closes in the key in which it began; thus, it is termed a *closed* section. It is, then, not dependent upon Part B for the completion of its tonal activity. Part B, however, is open. Its final cadence, though quite strong, is in G-sharp minor, the dominant minor of the key in which the section began.

These tonal relationships may not be specifically reflected in other ternary structures. They are typical, however, of a tonal design that supports the principle of contrast. The independence of Part B is reinforced by the closed tonal structure of Part A. Further, the return of Part A as the third section is reinforced by the open structure of Part B.

Part A of Example 5.3 is a phrase group in which alternating phrases confirm tonic, then dominant. The music from m. 31 to m. 47 is primarily terminative in function. The structural phenomena that define these divisions are largely cadential. Part B is also a phrase group, somewhat more stable tonally, whose final phrase (mm. 61–69) modulates to G-sharp minor. In each case, the nature of the vocal line obscures the cadences that produce the phrases.

The internal organization of the main divisions of ternary structures is not amenable to generalization, since it varies widely according to medium, genre, or historical context. However, the functional, motivic, and tonal attributes that reinforce the essential principle of contrast are more likely to be reflected in other examples of the form.

Example 5.3 obviously represents a more mature expression of the ternary principle in a vocal medium than Examples 5.1 and 5.2, although they are clearly products of the same principle. In the Classic period, simple ternary structures are relatively rare. In the nineteenth century, ternary structures are found most typically in moderately short instrumental pieces.

Example 5.4 Schumann: *Album for the Young,* Op. 68, No. 9, "Little Folk Song"

In Example 5.4, Part A, in D minor, is an eight-measure, symmetrical, parallel period. Part B, mm. 9–16, consists of two four-measure phrases, both of which end with a half-cadence in D major. Contrast essential to the ternary principle is provided in m. 9 by changes in modality, tempo, rhythm, and motive. Measures 17–24 represent a varied repetition of the first eight measures in D minor.

The cadential organization of the main divisions reflects the tonal principles observed in earlier examples.

Example 5.5 contains the kind of expansion of the basic ternary structure that is frequently associated with nineteenth-century expressions of the form.

Example 5.5   Chopin: Mazurka in F minor, Op. 63, No. 2

Example 5.5 *(cont.)*

Part A (mm. 1–16), a symmetrical, parallel period in F minor, represents a tonally closed expository section typical of ternary structures.

NOTE

1. The first phrase, closing with a half-cadence in m. 8, may be perceived in two four-measure units, the second of which is slightly developmental in function. The second phrase suggests no such subdivision and is continuous to its authentic cadence in m. 16.
2. The D-flat major chord in first inversion at the end of m. 16 serves as a *pivot* between the F minor tonality of Part A and the A-flat major section that follows.

Changes in tonality, accompaniment style, and motivic content provide the essential contrast for Part B. The first phrase, which again may be perceived in smaller units, begins clearly in A-flat major. Its cadence, in m. 24, suggests a half-cadence in C minor, or V of V in F minor. The function of the phrase, then, is partially transitional. Measures 25–33 represent a slightly varied repetition of the first phrase.

Measures 33–40 are clearly developmental and transitional in function. The expected return to F minor, suggested by the dominant harmony in m. 38, is evaded in the two measures that follow. The section concludes with a cadence on a tonally ambiguous A-flat major chord.

The clearly defined transitional passage that concludes Part B, and its relatively complex cadential organization, are logical expansions of the open tonal structure typical of other analogous sections.

NOTE

Many similar structures contain tonally closed B sections. Some form of transition, however, is typical. The tonal organization of middle sections in nineteenth-century ternary structures is less predictable than those of previous periods.

Part A is restated in mm. 41–56, completing the ternary design.

The ternary principle in a twentieth-century piece is shown in Example 5.6.

Example 5.6   Prokofiev: Badinage, Op. 3, No. 2. Used by permission of G. Schirmer, Inc.

Example 5.6 (cont.)

The music is organized in three main sections. Part A occupies mm. 1–10; Part B, mm. 11–24; and the return of Part A, mm. 25–34. Following the cadence in m. 10, contrast between Parts A and B is achieved by changes in tonality (from C to F), texture, density, dynamics, articulation, and register. The return of a modified form of Part A is signaled by a *ritardando*, following which the material that was first heard in m. 7 is restated. Parts A and B are also perceived as having contrasting structural functions. The former is largely expository, whereas the latter, in which fragmentation and transposition are exploited, is very clearly developmental.

EXERCISES

Apply the instructions for analysis to each of the following pieces.

1. Listen several times to the music provided.

2. On the score, mark the conclusion of each cadence with a bracket, and indicate its type and the key at that point.

3. List changes (if any) in tonality, tempo, meter, and so on that create structural phenomena.

4. Describe the organization of the three parts. First, answer the following questions individually in note form. Then, write a short paragraph that demonstrates your understanding of the ternary principle as it applies to this piece of music.

    a. What are the important structural phenomena?

    b. What is the key and cadence scheme?

    c. How are the structural units organized?

    d. What is the structural function of each unit?

    e. How is contrast achieved in Part B?

    f. Is the repeat of Part A literal or varied?

1. Schumann: *Myrthen,* Op. 25, No. 1, "Dedication"
   (Wennerstrom, pp. 318–322)

2. Chopin: Mazurka in G major, Op. 67, No. 1
   (Wennerstrom, pp. 343–344)

3. Brahms: Romance in F major, Op. 118, No. 5
   (Wennerstrom, pp. 371–374)

4. Schumann: *Waldszenen,* Op. 82, No. 7, "The Prophetic Bird"
   (Burkhart, pp. 347–349)

5. Chopin: Mazurka in G minor, Op. posth. 67, No. 2
   (Burkhart, pp. 364–365)

6. Handel: *Rinaldo,* "Lascia ch'io pianga"
   (Burkhart, pp. 101–103)

7. Chopin: Prelude in F-sharp major, Op. 28, No. 13
   (Turek, pp. 494–495)

8. Chopin: Mazurka in A minor, Op. 17, No. 4
   (Turek, pp. 504–507)

9. Bartók: *Mikrokosmos,* No. 128, "Peasant Dance"
   (Turek, pp. 808–810)

10. Tchaikovsky: *The Nutcracker,* "Dance of the Toy Flutes"
    (Norton Scores II, pp. 519–530)

Composite Ternary Form

A composite form is one in which smaller forms are clearly perceived in the articulation of the larger form's structure. The composite ternary form in the Baroque and Classic periods, for instance, was very often the result of the composition of two back-to-back binary dance movements, the first of which was literally repeated. Example 5.7, a minuet and trio, is typical of composite ternary movements of the Classic period.

Example 5.7   Haydn: Sonata in E-flat major, Hob.XVI/28, II

Example 5.7 *(cont.)*

Menuet da Capo

The movement's composite form is the result of a Menuet in rounded binary, a Trio in simple binary, and the repeat (Menuet da Capo) of the Menuet. In both of the interior forms, the binary principle is clearly expressed. Part A of the Menuet is a modulating period, the second phrase being extended from m. 8 to the double bar. Part B begins with some tonal uncertainty. The tonic, however, is solidly reestablished by m. 20, where the rounding-out process starts. The Trio, in the parallel minor mode, is made up of two indivisible modulating sections, both eight measures in length. The original thematic material is not restated in Part B.

NOTE

1. Contrast between the Trio and the Menuet is created primarily by a change from E-flat major to E-flat minor. Changes also, however, in phrase structure, motive, and rhythmic organization give additional assistance in the perception of the Trio as a contrasting musical entity.

2. In most composite ternary movements of the Baroque and Classic periods, Part B is a closed tonal unit.

EXERCISES

Apply the instructions for analysis to each of the following pieces.

1. Listen several times to the music provided.

2. On the score, mark the conclusion of each cadence with a bracket, and indicate its type and the key at that point.

3. List changes (if any) in tonality, tempo, meter, and so on that create structural phenomena.

4. Describe the internal organization of each of the three parts and the relationships among the parts. First, answer the following questions individually in note form. Then, write a short paragraph that demonstrates your understanding of the ternary principle as it applies to this piece of music.

    a. What are the important structural phenomena?

    b. What is the key and cadence scheme?

    c. How are the structural units organized?

    d. What is the structural function of each unit?

    e. What is the structural type of each part?

    f. How is contrast achieved in Part B?

    g. Is the repeat of Part A literal or varied?

    1. Beethoven: Sonata in E major, Op. 14, No. 1, II
       (Wennerstrom, pp. 233–234)

    2. Brahms: Intermezzo in A major, Op. 76, No. 6
       (Wennerstrom, pp. 366–369)

    3. Ravel: *Le Tombeau de Couperin*, No. 5, Menuet
       (Wennerstrom, pp. 418–421)

    4. Beethoven: Sonata in F minor, Op. 2, No. 1, III
       (Burkhart, pp. 264–265)

    5. Brahms: Intermezzo in A major, Op. 118, No. 2
       (Burkhart, pp. 399–402)

    6. Mozart: Serenade in C minor, K. 388, III
       (Burkhart, pp. 221–223)

    7. Mozart: String Quintet in G minor, K. 516, II
       (Turek, pp. 365–367)

    8. Haydn: String Quartet No. 21, Op. 9, No. 3, II
       (Turek, pp. 287–288)

9. Mozart: *Eine kleine Nachtmusik*, III, Menuetto and Trio
(Norton Scores I, pp. 493–494)

In addition, the Minuet and Trio movements of sonatas from the Classic period may profitably be studied.

6
imitative
procedures

INTRODUCTION

The musical texture created by the interaction of two or more *independent melodic lines* is termed *contrapuntal*. Music in which some or all melodic elements are fused by rhythm or contour is described as *homophonic*. *Polyphonic*, or "many-voiced," music may exhibit features of either or both of these textural types. The imitative procedures with which this chapter is concerned are primarily contrapuntal in texture.

Pieces of music whose organization is governed by the technique of *motivic imitation* among independent voices adhere to the principle of *statement and continuous development.*

While the technique of imitation has been a feature of contrapuntal music since the thirteenth century, the consistent use of the technique to organize the perceived parts of a piece is a more recent phenomenon.

Example 6.1 is a twelfth-century piece that shows the principle as the organizational force of a single section of a larger work.

Example 6.1 Hugo de Lantins: "Ce ieusse fait," Rondeau (first section). From
Historical Anthology of Music, Vol. I. Copyright © 1946, 1949 by
the President and Fellows of Harvard College: renewed 1974 by
Alice D. Humez and Willi Apel. Reprinted by permission of
Harvard University Press.

In this section, imitation occurs mainly between the two upper voices. The middle voice, through the downbeat of m. 5, represents the *statement* upon which the first phrase of the text is organized. The upper voice, in imitation a perfect fifth above, represents the *development* of the motive. The phrase concludes with a cadence on F in both voices in m. 9 of the upper voice. (The relationship between the voices after the downbeat of m. 7 remains contrapuntal but *free* of imitative development.)

The next phrase of text is organized by two *points of imitation*. The middle voice in its ninth measure is imitated by the upper voice for two measures. After a weak cadence in its fourteenth measure, the middle voice begins a three-measure statement, imitated by the upper voice an octave above.

While phrases are perceived through cadential phenomena, it is clear that the motives that begin the phrases, and their subsequent development through imitation, are essential to the organization of the phrases.

NOTE

1. Although the music within phrases cannot be said to be tonally developmental in this style, the imitative nature of much of the phrase content is perceived as motivically developmental.

2. Phrase organization in this piece is partially governed by the text. The imitative points are clearly related to textual divisions.

3. The rhythmic continuity at cadence points makes this structural phenomenon difficult to perceive. Typically, contrapuntal music does not produce the balanced, clear-cut phrase relationships of homophonic styles.

In Example 6.2, the absence of text clarifies the importance of the imitative procedure in organizing the phrase.

Example 6.2   Isaac: Instrumental Canzona (sixteenth century), mm. 1–6. From *Historical Anthology of Music,* Vol. I. Copyright © 1946, 1949 by the President and Fellows of Harvard College; renewed 1974 by Alice D. Humez and Willi Apel. Reprinted by permission of Harvard University Press.

This opening phrase, beginning in G, concludes with a cadence on D in m. 6. Its function, then, is partly transitional.

The statement, in the highest voice, is complete on the third quarter note of m. 4. The lowest voice, imitating at the octave below, and the middle voice at the perfect fourth below, represent the motivic development that completes the phrase.

In this example, the completion of the middle voice's imitative entrance on the third quarter note of m. 6 coincides with the cadence. Thus, the entire phrase illustrates the principle of statement and continuous development. The musical material of the first two voices that follows the imitated motive is free, but is related to the motive, and can be said to contribute to the perception of developmental function.

NOTE

While Example 6.2 does not yet illustrate the tonal development of later styles, the entrance of the middle voice on the dominant note has a clear tonal effect on the cadence that concludes the phrase.

While the principle of statement and continuous development governed the organization of much of the music of the Renaissance, the Baroque produced instrumental works of much greater tonal and motivic cohesiveness. The inventions and the fugues of J. S. Bach represent some of the most highly organized examples of such works.

Invention

Invention is the generally accepted name given to a number of imitative works in two or three voices (or parts) by J. S. Bach. They are examples of complete pieces governed by the principle of statement and continuous development.

In earlier examples, the principle typically governed sections of larger works, whose other structural units may or may not have been imitative. In addition, each of these imitative sections used different motivic materials. The inventions of Bach, however, exploit more limited motivic resources through the entire work.

It must be stressed that the invention and other works governed by imitative techniques are not *structures;* rather, they are *singular* structural expressions of the principle. They differ, often dramatically, from one another in the particulars of the relationships of their structural units. They are best termed, then, *imitative procedures.*

Example 6.3 J. S. Bach: Two-Part Invention in C major

Example 6.3 is divided, primarily by cadential phenomena, into three main sections. The first concludes with a perfect authentic cadence in G major on the downbeat of m. 7, the second with a perfect authentic cadence in A minor on the downbeat of m. 15, and the third with a perfect authentic cadence in C major in the last measure.

The three relatively balanced structural divisions may be thought of as phrases, but because of their fragmented, developmental quality, they are more properly termed *sections*. This specific sectional subdivision, as was mentioned earlier, is not necessarily typical of inventions in general. What are typical, however, are the tonal movement of each section toward a relatively stable cadence in a related key and the return of the tonic in the final section. Each section, then, is both developmental and transitional in function.

Section 1 begins with a statement of the invention's primary motive in the upper voice. It is imitated in the lower voice at the octave below in the second half of the measure. The upper voice in the second half of the measure contains an eighth-note motive with sufficient melodic importance to be considered separately (Example 6.3a).

Example 6.3a   Motivic Units

NOTE

The rhythmic character of motive 1 leads to the inclusion of the first eighth note of motive 2. The two motives can be said to be elided at that point.

In the second measure, each voice contains a repetition of the first measure at a different pitch level. The measure is called, then, a *sequence* of the first measure a perfect fifth higher. (A glossary of terms will be found on page 115.) These measures, containing the primary motives in the tonic key, constitute the *exposition* of the invention.

The continuous development that follows consists of *sequential* manipulations of primary motivic material, reaching the key of G major in the middle of m. 5 and extending to a convincing cadence at the end of the section.

The upper voice in mm. 3 and 4 contains four sequential statements of motive 1 with the intervals reversed in direction. This developmental technique is termed *inversion* (Example 6.3b).

Example 6.3b Inversion

NOTE

The last interval of the inversion is a second rather than the expected perfect fifth. The interval is said to be *contracted*.

The lower voice contains eighth-note figures that may be related to motive 2. The rhythmic grouping suggested by the melodic contour, however, causes them to be perceived as sequentially stated *fragments* of motive 1 with their note values doubled. The technique is termed *augmentation* (Example 6.3c).

Example 6.3c Augmentation

NOTE

The final statement, beginning on the second eighth note of m. 4, is *extended* to the downbeat of m. 5.

Measure 5 contains motive 1 in the lower voice, followed by an augmented fragment of motive 1. The upper voice in the first half of the measure contains a figure not strictly related to primary motives. It is followed by an inversion of motive 1 that is extended through the first two beats of m. 6 by sequential statements of the second fragment of motive 1. The final two beats of m. 6 contain free cadential material in each voice.

The second section opens with two measures that are analogous to the opening measures of the invention. Because they are expository in G major and contain complete versions of primary motives in their original form, these measures may be described as a *reexposition*. The exchange of parts (the lower voice contains material originally found in the upper voice) is known as *textural inversion*.

Measures 9 and 10 contain inversions of motive 1 in both voices. In addition, the lower voice contains a modification of motive 2 that shows the reversal of the order of the intervals. The statement is called a *retrograde* (Example 6.3d).

Example 6.3d   Retrograde

NOTE

The final interval is contracted.

Measures 11–14 are essentially a textural inversion of mm. 3–6. The cadential figure is similar to that of m. 6.

Unlike the second section, the third section does not begin with a reexposition, nor does it remain stable in the key of A minor. Measures 15 and 16 contain inversions and original versions of motive 1. Measures 17 and 18 contain sequences of mm. 15 and 16. Measures 19 and 20 contain sequential treatments of motive 1 in the upper voice, with *inverted augmentations* of the first fragment of motive 1 in the lower voice. The cadential figure in the upper voice at the end of m. 20 causes mm. 21 and 22 to be perceived as a *cadential extension.*

NOTE

The emphasis on the subdominant key in the third section is typical of the harmonic style and helps prepare the dominant that secures the return of the tonic.

Summary

The invention just cited is an example of a complete piece whose organization is governed by the statement of short primary motives and the development, primarily by imitative techniques, of those motives throughout the piece.

The structure of this invention may be described as sectional. Further, each section has as a harmonic goal a key closely related to the tonic. The last section returns to the tonic key.

In this case, virtually every note is related to the primary motives through readily perceived contrapuntal manipulation. The developmental function through which the principle is fulfilled is exceptionally clear.

The particulars of the structure of this invention may not be shared by others that share the principle of organization. Inventions, however, do have certain features in common as matters of style. These features are

1. Initial statement of short primary motives.
2. Continuous development of those motives by contrapuntal imitative techniques.
3. Tonal movements to related keys.
4. Structural divisions perceived through cadence.
5. Return to the tonic near the end.

EXERCISES

Study the analytical model, and apply the instructions for analysis to each of the following pieces.

1. Listen several times to the music provided.

2. On the score, mark the conclusion of each cadence with a bracket, and indicate its type and the key at that point. Use uppercase letters for major keys, lowercase for minor keys.

3. List changes (if any) in tonality, tempo, meter, and so on that create structural phenomena.

4. Describe the organization of the invention by answering the following questions.

    a. Which measures contain the exposition of the primary motive(s)?

    b. What are the main sections of the invention? What important structural phenomena clarify their perception?

    c. Are there reexpositions of the primary motives in later sections of the invention?

    d. What key areas are harmonic goals for the main structural units?

    e. In what measure does the tonic return?

5. Describe and locate by measure number important developmental techniques.

Analytical Model   J. S. Bach: Two-Part Inventions, No. 13 in A minor

Analytical Model *(cont.)*

Measures 1–2 contain the exposition of the primary motives. The upper voice in the first half of m. 1 is imitated at the octave below in the lower voice. The same procedure is followed in the second measure. The eighth-note figure that follows the initial statement is not imitated strictly. The primary motive is heard as being complete on the eighth note C on the third beat of m. 1.

The first section of the invention is complete on the third beat of m. 6. The authentic cadence in C major and a change in density help define the section.

The second section ends with an authentic cadence in E minor on the third beat of m. 13. A change in density again marks the division.

The third section ends on the downbeat of m. 18. While no strong cadence marks this division, the motivic structural phenomenon in the remainder of m. 18 reinforces the perception of a new section at this point.

There are reexpositions of the primary motive in mm. 6–8 (in C major), in m. 18 (in A minor), and in m. 22 (in A minor).

The harmonic goals of the sections are C major, E minor, and A minor. The tonic returns in m. 18.

Measure 3 in the upper voice contains a variation of the primary sixteenth-note motive in which some of the intervals are inverted and contracted, followed by the eighth-note figure similarly varied. Measure 4 contains a sequence of m. 3 in the upper voice. Measure 5 contains four fragments of the primary motive. Measures 14–17 include sequences of the variation of the primary motive first used in m. 3. The first three sixteenth notes are an inversion of the fragment in that measure. In each case, the figure is extended to the fourth beat of the measure. Measure 23 includes sequences of the second fragment of the primary motive in the upper voice and sequences of the second fragment of the eighth-note figure in the lower voice.

1. J. S. Bach: Two-Part Inventions, No. 14 in B-flat major
   (Wennerstrom, pp. 88–89)

2. J. S. Bach: Three-Part Sinfonia No. 9 in F minor
   (Wennerstrom, pp. 89–91)

3. J. S. Bach: Two-Part Inventions, No. 9 in F minor
   (Burkhart, p. 122)

4. Bartók: *Mikrokosmos*, Vol. 4, No. 101, "Diminished Fifth"
   (Burkhart, p. 482)

5. J. S. Bach: Two-Part Inventions, No. 6 in E major and No. 9 in F minor
   (Turek, pp. 153–156)

In addition, the rest of the Two-Part Inventions and Three-Part Sinfonias of Bach may be profitably studied.

A number of the preludes from *The Well-Tempered Clavier* of Bach are examples of inventions.

Book 1: 13 in F-sharp major, 14 in F-sharp minor, 17 in A-flat major.
Book 2: 24 in B minor.

Fugue

The fugue is considered to be a compositional type whose organization, possibly more than any other, systematically exploits the principle of statement and continuous development. Because of the prevalence of imitative techniques, it may be likened to the invention. In the hands of J. S. Bach, the fugue reached a degree of sophistication and maturity that earned it a special place in the history of contrapuntal musical genres. It may be safely stated that since Bach's death, with several notable exceptions, the fugue has not been treated as a serious, creative form of composition.

The fugue is *essentially* a contrapuntal composition that is constructed of a given number of voices (usually three or four, but sometimes two, five, or six) and that follows no predictable formal pattern. It is based upon a theme, or *subject,* that intermittently recurs in the various voices at different pitch levels and in different keys as the composition unfolds. As in the invention, the exploitation of developmental techniques such as inversion and sequence is typically encountered.

Although a fugue may sometimes exhibit resemblances to a number of forms already studied, it is best understood in terms of *motivic development* within a wide variety of *tonal frameworks*. These tonal frameworks are frequently perceived in three main sections.

1. *Expository section:* This section, which is analogous to the exposition of the invention, is primarily expository in function, with secondary developmental function.
2. *Modulatory section:* This section's functions are mainly transitional and developmental, but expository function is frequently encountered.
3. *Closing section:* While this section is largely terminative in function, expository function is commonly found.

It must be stressed again that, like the invention, each fugue is a singular expression of the principle of statement and continuous development. Fugues differ dramatically from one another in terms of the nature of their subjects, in the specific tonal relationships contained in their expository sections, and in the particulars of the relationships between their structural units. Thus, no single fugue can be considered a model, nor can it exemplify all the features associated with the genre.

Example 6.4 is written in three voices (soprano, alto, and bass) and can be considered a typical expression of the structural principle.

Example 6.4   J. S. Bach: *W.T.C.*, Vol. I, Fugue 21 in B-flat major

Example 6.4 *(cont.)*

The *expository section* of this fugue (often termed *exposition*) concludes on the downbeat of m. 17; the tonal activity is entirely in the keys of B-flat major and its dominant, F major. The *modulatory section,* mm. 17–41 (downbeat), exploits the keys of G minor, C minor, and E-flat major. The *closing section,* in B-flat major, occupies the remainder of the fugue. The second and third main sections are initiated by elided cadences.

Section One: Expository Section

The exposition begins with a *subject* in the soprano voice that comes to rest on the downbeat of the fifth measure. It is constructed of two contrasting melodic units, each lasting two measures.

Example 6.4a   Motivic Unit 1

NOTE

The second measure is an *ornamented sequence* of the first.

Example 6.4b   Motivic Unit 2

NOTE

The fourth measure is a *varied repetition* of the third.

In m. 5, with the exception of the first note, the subject is restated in the alto voice at the interval of a perfect fourth lower. Such a restatement (either up a fifth or down a fourth) is referred to as an *answer.* Furthermore, if the restatement is exact, the answer is termed *real;* if the restatement is modified, the answer is termed *tonal.* This is a tonal answer, because the first note of the answer is written a *perfect fifth below* the first note of the subject. Such a modification serves to prolong the tonic key and to make the movement of the answer to the dominant tonally less abrupt. Meanwhile, the soprano voice consists of a contrapuntal line whose main points of interest, in this case, are the tied notes at the end of mm. 5 and 6 and the repeated notes in mm. 7 and 8. It can be seen, too, that the second measure is loosely derived from the inversion of the beginning of the subject and that the first beat of the last measure (m. 8) is an exact transposition of the subject at that point. Such a line, when systematically used in conjunction with the subject, is termed a *countersubject*. Following the weak cadence in F major in m. 9, the subject is heard in the bass voice, the countersubject in the alto voice, and a somewhat more fragmented second countersubject in the soprano. In mm. 13–17, the answer is stated in the soprano, the second countersubject in the alto, and the first in the bass.

The section as a whole may be subdivided into smaller sections that coincide with the entries of the subject or the answer in mm. 5, 9, and 13, all of which follow weak authentic cadences. Furthermore, the increase in density in mm. 5 and 9 reinforces the perception of these points as being structurally significant. From a tonal standpoint, the role of the exposition is primarily expository and secondarily developmental—the musical activity is expressed exclusively in the tonic and the dominant keys. Motivically, the perception of development is unmistakable—the subject and the two countersubjects share several contours with respect to both pitch and rhythm.

Section Two: Modulatory Section

The modulatory section of a fugue is typically made up of *episodes* and *reexpositions*. An episode is often sequential or imitative or both, and usually exploits motivic material first encountered in the exposition. A *complete* statement of the subject is not heard during an episode. A reexposition comprises at least one complete statement of the subject or the answer in any voice.

The episode that begins this section in m. 17 features a rapid modulation to G minor, the first two measures being a textural inversion of mm. 15 and 16. In m. 19, a three-measure descending sequence is initiated that demonstrates the principle of continuous development. The soprano voice is based upon the last full measure of the fugue's subject, while the bass is its first measure in inversion. This section of the episode is clearly marked by a change in density.

In m. 22, following a half-cadence, the first reexposition begins with a change in register. The subject is presented (still in G minor) in the alto, while the soprano and the bass state the first and the second countersubjects respectively. This statement of the subject is followed in m. 26 by the subject in C minor in the bass, once again accompanied by the two countersubjects.

The second episode, articulated by another change in density, starts at the beginning of m. 30 in the key of C minor. Its first three measures are very closely derived from the first three measures of the first episode (mm. 19–21); the bass and the soprano are interchanged, and a skeletal alto voice has been added. In m. 33, a textural inversion of mm. 30–32 begins.

In m. 35, it appears as if another reexposition in C minor is about to begin. The materials in the soprano, alto, and bass voices represent, respectively, the first countersubject, the subject (or the answer), and the second countersubject. In mm. 35–36, however, a modulation to E-flat major takes place, and a proper second reexposition is introduced in m. 37 with the subject in the soprano, followed by an answer in the alto in m. 41. The two countersubjects are again present.

Section Three: Terminative Section

The terminative section of a fugue functions to reaffirm the tonic key and to bring the work to conclusion.

In this fugue, the answer (m. 41) to the reexposition in E-flat is used to reaffirm the tonic (B-flat being E-flat's dominant). Following the end of the answer on the downbeat of m. 45, for two measures the three voices are involved in a textural inversion of mm. 43–44. The effect is to create tension through a dominant extension that is finally resolved at the end.

The very strong emphasis on tonic and dominant harmony, particularly in the last seven measures of this fugue, lend to this section a strong perception of terminative function. Such a perception is complemented by the absence of any new developmental devices.

Summary

Although it has been demonstrated that this fugue may be perceived in three main sections, each of which has a specific tonal role, it must be emphasized that the primary organizing principle of the fugue is one of statement and continuous development. The subject, sometimes in its entirety and sometimes in fragmentation, is treated throughout both imitatively and sequentially. In addition, both countersubjects contain motives that are obviously derived from parts of the subject. Thus, the generating force of the fugue is the result of perpetual contrapuntal motivic manipulation.

Analyses of other fugues are unlikely to unveil structures in which the details of the internal organization of the sections match this one. For instance, the exposition may contain a greater or a smaller number of entries of the subject or the answer; a systematic use of countersubject material may or may not be present; the tonal excursions in the modulatory section may be more or less elaborate; the terminative section may be longer and may feature more complex contrapuntal manipulations. However, this fugue, like the invention discussed earlier, does contain a number of features that tend to be associated with the style in general.

1. An initial statement of a subject that, through its motivic and rhythmic structure, gives the fugue its special characteristics.
2. An imitative reiteration of the subject (or the answer) that serves to establish the principal tonality.
3. A continuous development of related motivic material by a variety of contrapuntal techniques.
4. Reiterations of the subject at various points throughout the fugue.
5. A reaffirmation of the tonic key toward the end.

Other Expressions of the Structural Principle

Fugato.   The term *fugato* applies to a section of a composition (other than a fugue) in which fugal imitative techniques are exploited.

Fughetta.   A fughetta is a short fugue that is typically limited with respect to tonal movement and contrapuntal activity.

Double Fugue.   A fugue in which two subjects are treated separately at first, then simultaneously, is termed a *double fugue.* (Fugues in which three or four subjects are similarly treated are termed *triple* or *quadruple fugues.*)

GLOSSARY

Augmentation: the use of larger note values for all or part of a motive.

Contraction: the reduction of the size of one or more intervals in a motive.

Diminution: the use of shorter note values for all or part of a motive.

Expansion: the enlargement of the size of one or more intervals in a motive.

Fragmentation: the use of a part of a motive.

Free counterpoint: melodic material in imitative textures not associated with previously established motives.

Imitation: the repetition of a motive or a fragment in a different voice.

Inversion: the reversal of the direction of the intervals in a motive.

Point of imitation: marks the beginning of a series of imitative entries in a contrapuntal composition.

Retrograde: the reversal of the order of the intervals in a motive.

Sequence: the repetition in the same voice of a motive or a fragment at a different pitch level.

Stretto: the overlapping imitation of subject and answer in a fugue.

Textural inversion: the repetition of a section of counterpoint in which the content of the voices is exchanged. (*Invertible counterpoint* occurs when textural inversion involves the lowest voice.)

EXERCISES

Study the analytical model, and apply the instructions for analysis to each of the following pieces.

1. Listen several times to the music provided.

2. On the score, mark the conclusion of each cadence with a bracket, and indicate its type and the key at that point. Use uppercase letters for major keys, lowercase for minor keys.

3. List changes (if any) in tonality, tempo, meter, and so on that create structural phenomena.

4. Identify all complete statements of the subject or the answer. Use "Sub" for the subject and "Ans" for the answer.

5. Identify all statements of the countersubject. Use "CS."

6. By measure number, identify the three main sections of the fugue and the important structural phenomena that articulate them.

7. Describe the organization of the expository section of the fugue by answering the following questions.

    a.   How many statements of subject and answer does the expository section contain?

    b.   Are there links, or bridges, between statements? What is their function?

    c.   Are statements of the answer tonal or real?

8. Describe the organization of the modulatory section of the fugue by answering the following questions.

    a.   Where are the episodes? What tonal activity is associated with them? What developmental techniques are exploited?

    b.   Where are the reexpositions? In what keys are they? What developmental techniques are exploited?

    c.   What structural phenomena help define episodes and reexpositions?

9. Describe the organization of the terminative section of the fugue by answering the following questions.

    a.   Is there a statement of the subject or the answer?

    b.   What developmental techniques are exploited?

    c.   How is terminative function expressed?

Analytical Model   J. S. Bach: *W.T.C.,* Vol. I, Fugue 11 in F major

Analytical Model *(cont.)*

The fugue is divided into three main sections. The expository section ends on the downbeat of m. 31 with a weak authentic cadence in F major. The modulatory section is complete on the downbeat of m. 64 with a similar weak cadence.

The expository section contains seven statements of the subject or the answer, the last in the alto overlapping the previous statement. Such overlapping imitation is termed *stretto*. There is a two-measure link between the answer and the entry of the subject in mm. 8–9 that returns the tonality to F major. A five-measure link in mm. 13–17 emphasizes the dominant note in preparation for the fourth entry of the subject. Both statements of the answer are tonal.

The first episode modulates from F major to D minor in mm. 31–36. The two upper voices, in sequence and in imitation, exploit a fragment from the third measure of the subject (itself an inversion of the second measure). The lower voice is derived from the inversion of the first measure of the subject. The second episode begins in G minor in m. 56 and modulates to the tonic in m. 64. Its construction is very similar to the first episode, although a textural inversion takes place in m. 60.

The first reexposition begins on the third beat of m. 36 in the key of D minor. Development is perceived largely through the use of stretti, in m. 38 in the alto and in m. 40 in the bass. The last entry of the subject is followed by an extension to a strong perfect authentic cadence in D minor in m. 46. A second reexposition in G minor follows. It is characterized by stretto entries in mm. 48 and 50. In each statement of the subject, the third measure is ornamented. In m. 50, the first note of the subject is disguised by the sixteenth-note ascending motion that precedes it. This reexposition concludes with a two-measure extension to a perfect authentic cadence in G minor on the downbeat of m. 56.

The first reexposition is articulated by a change in register following a half-cadence in D minor in m. 36. The second reexposition follows a strong authentic cadence in D minor and is further defined by a change in texture. The second episode is marked by the authentic cadence in G minor in m. 56.

The terminative section contains an ornamented statement of the subject, beginning in m. 64 in the soprano. The developmental techniques are imitation (mm. 66 and 67), fragmentation in the bass voice, and ornamentation of the fragments in the soprano (mm. 68 and 69). Tonal terminative function is confined largely to the last five measures of the fugue.

1. J. S. Bach: *The Well-Tempered Clavier*, Vol. I, Fugue 15 in G major
   (Wennerstrom, pp. 91–95)

2. J. S. Bach: *The Well-Tempered Clavier*, Vol. II, Fugues 9 in E major, 16 in G minor
   (Wennerstrom, pp. 98–100, 106–110)

3. J. S. Bach: *The Well-Tempered Clavier*, Vol. I, Fugues 1 in C major, 2 in C minor, 16 in G minor
   (Burkhart, pp. 125–128, 133–134)

4. J. S. Bach: *The Well-Tempered Clavier*, Vol. I, Fugues 17 in A-flat major, 22 in B-flat minor
   (Turek, pp. 196–198, 201–203)

5. J. S. Bach: Organ Fugue in G minor (Little)
   (Norton Scores I, pp. 185–189)

In addition, several of the remaining fugues in *The Well-Tempered Clavier* may be appropriate for study. Some good examples are Vol. I: Nos. 7, 12, 20, 23, and 24; and Vol. II: Nos. 1, 2, 5, 6, 7, 10, 11, 12, 17, 19, 20, 21, and 24.

7

variation procedures

INTRODUCTION

A variation is simply a restatement of any musical entity that retains some elements of the original and changes others. The variation procedures assembled for analysis in this chapter are governed by the principle of *statement and modified repetition.*

Example 7.1, based on the statement and three repetitions of an eight-measure melodic phrase (often termed *cantus firmus*), can be said to be at least partially organized by the repetitions of the melody in the lowest voice. The *variations* are perceived in the melodic activity of the other voices.

Example 7.1 Motet, On parole—A Paris—Frèse nouvele (thirteenth century).
From *Historical Anthology of Music,* Vol. I. Copyright © 1946,
1949 by the President and Fellows of Harvard College; renewed
1974 by Alice D. Humez and Willi Apel. Reprinted by permission
of Harvard University Press.

Extended instrumental works governed by the principle are more recent phenomena. Example 7.2 illustrates clearly the principle of statement and modified repetition.

Example 7.2 Scheidt: "Wehe, Windgen, wehe"; Theme and Keyboard
Variations 1, 2, 4. From *Historical Anthology of Music,* Vol. II.
Copyright © 1950 by the President and Fellows of Harvard
College; renewed 1978 by Alice D. Humez and Willi Apel.
Reprinted by permission of Harvard University Press.

2. Variatio

4. Variatio

Example 7.2 *(cont.)*

The *statement,* or "theme," is a ten-measure asymmetrical period. The melody, in the upper voice, is simply harmonized in chorale style. It is followed by a series of repetitions, or "variations," each with a distinct character. In the first variation, an imitative, contrapuntal texture replaces the homophonic texture of the theme; the melody and the harmony are essentially unchanged. Variation 2 involves an ornamentation of the melody in the upper voice, while the original harmonies and texture are retained. In the fourth variation, the melody of the theme is placed in the lower voice of a two-voiced texture; a countermelody in the upper voice suggests a slightly more complex harmonic scheme.

Procedures organized by the uninterrupted repetition of a short melodic or harmonic unit (such as Example 7.1) are termed *continuous variations.* Those whose themes and variations are closed, complete structural units (such as Example 7.2) are termed *sectional variations.*

Continuous Variations

The sixteenth through early eighteenth centuries represent the height of the development of continuous variation procedures based upon the earlier cantus firmus principle. These procedures tend to fall into two types: those based upon a single melodic unit (generally found in the bass) and those based upon a harmonic progression. The former are appropriately called *ground bass* or *basso ostinato.* The terms *chaconne* and *passacaglia* have been applied to both types, although *chaconne* in particular is more commonly associated with the latter. Examples 7.3 and 7.4 illustrate attributes associated with continuous variations.

Example 7.3a   J. S. Bach: Passacaglia in C minor, mm. 1–32

Example 7.3a *(cont.)*

This passacaglia is based upon twenty uninterrupted repetitions of the bass melody in mm. 1–8. Each iteration concludes with authentic cadential movement. Measures 9–32 (Example 7.3a) represent three variations, the first two of which are characterized by dotted rhythms and by ornamented suspensions on the first beat of each measure. The third variation is, by contrast, characterized by imitative eighth-note figures in the upper voices. This combination of stability and constant change persists throughout the piece and represents the organizing principle of continuous variation compositions.

Example 7.3b   Measures 40–48

In the fifth variation (Example 7.3b), the bass melody is ornamented so that it becomes a part of the imitative texture begun in the upper voices in m. 40. The same technique may be observed in the ninth variation.

Example 7.3c Measures 89–96

In the eleventh variation (Example 7.3c), the theme appears in the upper voice. The same is true of the twelfth variation.

In contrast to the passacaglia, Example 7.4 is based upon a repeated harmonic progression.

Example 7.4 Fischer: *Melponene* Suite, Chaconne

This chaconne consists of eight iterations of a four-measure harmonic progression whose basic movement is from tonic to dominant. Although the bass line plays a prominent role in articulating the harmonic structure, it can be seen that it is not featured alone, nor is it the same throughout.

Measures 1–4 feature a simple melody over the basic harmonic progression. In the following four measures, the music is repeated almost exactly. Similarly, mm. 9–12 and mm. 13–16 feature more elaborate melodic iterations over essentially the same harmonic pattern.

In mm. 17–20, the harmonic pattern is altered, and the melodic emphasis is shifted to the lower voices. Measures 21–24 are a slightly varied repetition of these measures.

In mm. 25–28, the melodic activity returns to the top voice, and the harmony is a decorated version of the original four measures. The chaconne concludes with more complex and slightly extended melodic and harmonic activity.

Summary

The principle of statement and modified repetition produces small structural divisions created by cadential phenomena associated with the theme. In the chaconne (Example 7.4), however, larger structural units are also easily identified. The pairs of variations, the changes in harmonic detail, and the shifts in melodic activity all contribute to the perception of the larger subdivisions of the structure. Similarly, study of the complete Bach passacaglia will reveal a sectional organization articulated by important structural phenomena. Like inventions and fugues, continuous variations are singular structural expressions of their organizing principle and thus differ dramatically in the details of their internal subdivisions. They do, however, have the following features in common:

1. The theme (bass melody or harmonic progression) is usually repeated throughout in the same key.
2. The process of variation is achieved by the changing character of elements other than the theme.
3. The theme may be melodically or harmonically altered or ornamented.
4. The theme may be subject to change in register.

EXERCISES

Apply the instructions for analysis to each of the pieces that follow.

1. Listen several times to the music provided.

2. On the score, mark the conclusion of each cadence with a bracket, and indicate its type and the key at that point. Use uppercase letters for major keys, lowercase for minor keys.

3. List changes (if any) in tonality, tempo, meter, and so on that create structural phenomena.

4. Determine whether the variations are based upon a bass melody or a chord progression.

5. Determine the length of the theme and how many times it is repeated.

6. For each repetition, determine whether the theme is present in its original form. If it is not, describe the nature of the alterations.

7. For each repetition, describe how the activity of other elements creates variation.

8. Evaluate the extent to which the composition may be perceived in larger structural units than those articulated by the theme itself. List important structural phenomena that contribute to this perception.

1. Purcell: *King Arthur,* Chaconne
   (Wennerstrom, pp. 78–81)

2. Handel: Chaconne in G major, Variations 1, 4, 62
   (Wennerstrom, pp. 122–123)

3. Britten: Serenade, Op. 31, "Dirge"
   (Wennerstrom, pp. 501–504)

4. Purcell: *Dido and Aeneas,* "Dido's Lament"
   (Burkhart, pp. 73–77; Norton Scores I, pp. 101–103)

5. J. S. Bach: Partita No. 2 in D minor for Violin Solo, Chaconne
   (Burkhart, pp. 114–120)

6. J. S. Bach: Mass in B minor, "Crucifixus"
   (Burkhart, pp. 137–141)

7. J. S. Bach: Passacaglia in C minor for Organ
   (Turek, pp. 158–165)

8. Franck: Prelude, Aria, and Finale, Prelude, mm. 84–124
   (Turek, pp. 609–611)

9. Monteverdi: *Zefiro torna,* Ciaccona
   (Norton Scores I, pp. 81–90)

Sectional Variations

In contrast to continuous variations, in which the theme is a short bass melody or a harmonic progression, the theme of sectional variations is a *complete* musical entity with melodic, harmonic, and rhythmic identity. In addition, the theme is typically of larger dimensions than a single phrase (periodic or binary structures are encountered commonly) and reaches a definite conclusion before the first variation begins. In the same manner, each variation is perceived as a self-contained musical unit. Although sectional variations may be found in the Baroque, they are much more widely associated with the Classic period. Such compositions, which exist independently or as part of larger works, are termed *theme and variations* (Example 7.5).

Example 7.5a Mozart: Sonata in A major, K. 331, I, Theme

The first eight measures of this rounded binary structure (Example 7.5a) represent a nonmodulating, symmetrical, parallel period. Part B is also periodic, the consequent phrase being extended by two measures. The theme is expository throughout and is characterized by simple diatonic melody and harmony and by clear phrase structure.

Example 7.5b   Variation I

Variation I (Example 7.5b) retains the phrase structure and the harmony of the theme. Variation is perceived in the ornamentation of the melody and in the changes in texture, dynamics, and rhythm. Variations such as this, in which the emphasis is on melodic elaboration, are termed *ornamental variations*.

Example 7.5c Variation III

Example 7.5c *(cont.)*

The most obvious modification in Variation III (Example 7.5c) is the change in mode. In addition, the melody is disguised by a series of sixteenth-note figures that prevail throughout. Texture and dynamics are again varied elements. The formal structure and the harmony remain essentially unchanged. Variations in which a melodic figure is systematically exploited are termed *figural variations*.

Example 7.5d   Variation VI

Example 7.5d *(cont.)*

The altered elements in Variation VI (Example 7.5d) are tempo, meter, melody, texture, and dynamics. The structure and the harmony of the theme are again retained. The variation is extended to include an eight-measure coda.

Summary

The structural divisions in procedures such as this are clearly dictated by the variations themselves. Larger structural divisions may be suggested by groupings of variations on the basis of common elements such as tempo, meter, and rhythm. While other examples of theme and variation compositions differ from Example 7.5 with reference to overall organization, there are certain features they tend to have in common.

1. The theme (particularly since the Classical period) is generally a binary structure.

2. There are variation techniques that are commonly exploited. These include melodic ornamentation; melodic figuration; melodic simplification (the representation of the theme's melody in skeletal form); changes in mode, meter, tempo; contrapuntal development; the use of attributes associated with other pieces, such as dance movements.

EXERCISES

Apply the instructions for analysis to each of the pieces that follow.

1. Listen several times to the music provided.

2. For the theme, mark with a bracket on the score the conclusion of each cadence, and indicate its type and the key at that point. Use uppercase letters for major keys, lowercase for minor keys.

3. For the theme, list changes (if any) in tonality, tempo, meter, and so on that create structural phenomena.

4. Describe the theme's structural organization (e.g., parallel period, rounded binary).

5. For each variation, list those elements of the theme that are retained and those that are varied. Describe how variation is achieved.

6. If appropriate, classify each variation as to type (e.g., figural, ornamental, simplifying, contrapuntal).

7. Identify structural units, if any, that do not constitute the theme or its variations. Describe the function of each in the composition (e.g., transition, extension, coda).

8. Evaluate the extent to which the composition may be perceived in larger structural units than those articulated by the theme itself. List common elements that contribute to the grouping of variations that create these structural units.

> **1.** J. S. Bach: Goldberg Variations, Aria and Variations 8, 15, 18, 30
> (Wennerstrom, pp. 111–117)
>
> **2.** Mozart: String Quartet in D minor, K. 421, IV
> (Wennerstrom, pp. 212–216)

3. Dello Joio: Piano Sonata No. 3, I
   (Wennerstrom, pp. 505–511)

4. Mozart: Sonata in D major, K. 284, III
   (Burkhart, pp. 195–205)

5. Stravinsky: Sonata for Two Pianos, II
   (Burkhart, pp. 505–514)

6. Handel: Suite No. 4 in D minor, Sarabande
   (Turek, pp. 248–249)

7. Schumann: Symphonic Etudes, Op. 13, Theme and Etudes 1, 2, 4, 7, 11
   (Turek, pp. 484–491)

8. Haydn: Symphony No. 104 in D major, II
   (Norton Scores I, pp. 337–350)

9. Schubert: Quintet in A major (*The Trout*), IV
   (Norton Scores II, pp. 8–23)

10. Beethoven: Sonata in G major, Op. 14, No. 2, II

11. Beethoven: Sonata in A-flat major, Op. 26, I

8

the binary principle:
sonata-allegro form

INTRODUCTION

The continued expansion of formal components associated with rounded binary movements (summarized in Chapter 4) eventually produced a stylized procedure known as *sonata-allegro form*. While such forms are generally longer than rounded binary structures, tonal and structural elements of the binary principle are reflected consistently.

Example 8.1, which represents an early version of this expanded form, illustrates several structural features associated with sonata-allegro form.

Example 8.1   Scarlatti: Sonata in C major, Longo 359. Used by permission of
G. Schirmer, Inc.

Example 8.1 *(cont.)*

Example 8.1 *(cont.)*

Measures 1–6, an extended phrase, are expository in function and represent an opening typically found in binary design.

Measures 7–21 are transitional in function. Modulation to the key of G major occurs in this section, and the fragmented motivic content is consistent with the section's function.

NOTE

In the shorter simple and rounded binary movements, an authentic cadence in the dominant signals the conclusion of Part A. The half-cadence here leads to an expansion of the second tonal area in the first part of the structure.

Measures 22–30 (downbeat) represent a second expository section that consists of two phrases in G major connected by an elided deceptive cadence in m. 26.

NOTE

This section is motivically distinct from the first two sections and exhibits an emphasis on the second key area in Part A not found in binary structures studied earlier.

The repetitive cadential activity in mm. 30–35 identifies this section as terminative in function. The end of the section, and of Part A, is marked clearly by an authentic cadence in G major.

Measures 36–50 are developmental in function. The keys of F major, D minor, and A minor are suggested prior to the section's conclusion with a half-cadence in C major.

NOTE

The fragmented references to motives found in Part A, as well as the unstable tonal atmosphere, are once again typical of the section that follows the double bar in smaller binary structures.

Measures 51–64 are almost exactly the same as mm. 22–35 transposed into the tonic key.

NOTE

The return to the tonic key is a typical binary procedure. However, the restatement of the thematic material from the second tonal area of Part A in the rounding-out process is a departure from the less complex designs, in which all the thematic material in Part A is usually derived from the opening few measures.

The movement, then, is divided into seven clearly identifiable sections—four in Part A and three in Part B. As in earlier examples of the binary structure, cadence is the most important structural phenomenon in the perception of the divisions of the form.

This Scarlatti sonata, while adhering to the tonal and basic functional design of the rounded binary structure, represents a larger, more complex expression of the binary principle. Specifically, the emphasis on musical materials leading to and encompassing the second key area in Part A and the corresponding references to some of the same materials in Part B cause an inevitable expansion of the binary design.

Sonata-Allegro Form

In Example 8.2, the sections are even more clearly articulated in an overall design that was standardized in the late eighteenth and early nineteenth centuries and that is labeled *sonata-allegro form*.

NOTE

Although most of the terminology associated with sonata-allegro form is standard, descriptive terms vary, particularly as they pertain to the smaller structural levels. The terminology employed here has been chosen because the authors consider it to be the most appropriate for the complete understanding of the form.

Example 8.2 Beethoven: Sonata in G major, Op. 49, No. 2, I

Example 8.2 *(cont.)*

Example 8.2 *(cont.)*

A cursory examination of the movement shows that the largest structural division occurs at the double bar between m. 52 and m. 53. The strong cadence in the key of the dominant in m. 52 suggests that this movement is divided in a fashion similar to many binary movements and that the typical tonal motion from tonic to related key (specifically, dominant) is reflected here as well. This principal division is called the *exposition*.

The exposition is divided into several smaller sections, defined primarily by function and tonality. In this example, mm. 1–12 are expository in function: The key of G major is established, and clear phrase structure is exhibited. Expository sections within the exposition are labeled *groups* and are assigned a number according to the order of their appearance. In this movement, then, mm. 1–12 are designated as *Group 1*.

Measures 13–14, motivically related to the third phrase of Group 1, serve as a bridge to a longer section (mm. 15–20) that is clearly marked by changes in dynamics and rhythmic content. This section exhibits the increased rhythmic activity and the fragmentary motivic content associated with transitional function and, in this case through a prolongation of the half-cadence on the downbeat of m. 15, prepares for the related key. The section is called the *transition*.

NOTE

In many cases, the transition effects a complete modulation to the related key. Whether the section modulates to the related key or, as in this example, simply emphasizes it, the term *transition* is appropriate. In most cases, the rhythmic and motivic attributes of transitional function are present if the tonal function is not clear.

Measures 21–36 are again expository in function. The tonality of D major is established, and the four phrases that constitute the double period reinforce the section's functional purpose. Because it is the second expository unit in the exposition, this section is termed *Group 2*.

NOTE

1. The thematic material in Group 2 differs from that in Group 1.
2. In m. 21, changes in dynamics and rhythm are significant structural phenomena in the perception of the new structural unit.

As a result of the reiterative cadential activity in D major, mm. 36–52 are clearly terminative in function and are thus designated by the term *closing section*.

NOTE

The prevailing rhythmic activity of the closing section is derived from the transition.

Measures 53–59 (downbeat) are developmental in function. The keys of D minor, A minor, and E minor are suggested, and altered versions of the motivic material from the transition and Group 2 are present. Measures 60–63 constitute a prolongation of the half-cadence in E minor with which the section concludes. With the elided cadence in m. 63, another short section begins. Its primary function is transitional; through a circle of fifths, the tonic is reestablished on the downbeat of m. 67. The term *development* is applied to the entire section between the double bar and the return of the tonic, although not all the material is necessarily developmental.

NOTE

In this case, alterations of previously heard motivic material are included in the development. In some development sections, however, the motivic material is less clearly related to the exposition; sometimes it is not related at all. What *is* fundamental to this section is the tonal instability that makes the return to the tonic a significant event. In this sense, the development is precisely analogous to the section directly following the double bar in smaller binary movements.

In mm. 67–70, a literal repetition of the first phrase of Group 1 of the exposition occurs. The coincidence of the return of opening motivic material with the return of the tonic key is typical of rounded binary designs and marks the beginning of the section designated *recapitulation* in sonata-allegro structures.

Typically, the recapitulation consists of the repetition, in some form, of the units that make up the exposition. A comparison, therefore, of the structural units in the recapitulation with those of the exposition reveals the nature of the section.

Measures 71–75 (downbeat) are derived from the second phrase of Group 2, but are altered to be partially transitional in function. The phrase ends with an authentic cadence in C major, the subdominant key. Measures 75–82 (downbeat) represent a transposed version of mm. 36–43, a part of the closing of the exposition. The function of this section, then, is heard at least partially as developmental. Its tonal function, however, is transitional. The section prepares a return of the transition from the exposition (mm. 15–20). Measures 82–87 again emphasize the tonality of the dominant. The entire section (mm. 71–87) typifies the expanded function of the transition within the recapitulation. The emphasis on C major (the subdominant) in the transition alters the perception of the tonal identity of the key of D major, which follows it. Here, D major is perceived more clearly as a potential dominant than as a new tonic.

NOTE

In this example, the recapitulation consists of a *shortened* version of Group 1 and an *extended and developed* version of the transition. Thus, the recapitulation is analogous to, but not a literal repetition of, the exposition. The relationships are typical of, but by no means standard for, sonata-allegro structures.

In mm. 88–103, Group 2 from the exposition is transposed to the tonic key. It can be seen that the effect of the transition in the recapitulation is different from that of the transition in the exposition. Typically, expository sections that established a related key in the exposition *maintain the tonic key* when repeated in the recapitulation. The purpose, then, of the transition in the recapitulation is to prepare this continuation of tonic as if it were a new tonality. For this reason, the transition is altered and generally lengthened in the recapitulation.

The closing section begins in m. 103 and continues to the end of the movement. With the exception of an interpolation (mm. 118–119), it is a literal transposition of the same section in the exposition. Its function, therefore, is also terminative.

The Binary Principle in Sonata-Allegro Form

The sonata-allegro, despite its expanded nature and the special terminology applied to its structural units, is yet another example of the tonal principles associated with binary structures. As in the case of rounded binary form, a motivic principle is involved, the return of the tonic in Part B being associated with a return of the original melodic/thematic material. Indeed, the term *recapitulation* implies a rather thorough expansion of the rounding-out process described earlier. Motivically, the link between the recapitulation and the exposition of sonata-allegro structures is far more specific than that of the rounding-out section of rounded binaries. Motive, then, as a structural phenomenon plays a critical role in the perception of the structural design in sonata-allegro movements.

In addition, the placement and the ordering of structural functions within sonata-allegro movements provide *functional principles* that are peculiar to the structure. The expansion of Part A results in the inclusion of at least two sections with expository function, each associated with a key of importance in the exposition. Typically, these expository sections, which usually consist of phrase groups or periods, are connected by a section with transitional function. The simple cadential activity in the second key area at the end of Part A is often represented by a section with terminative function. Although the primary function of the section before the return of the tonic key in Part B is transitional, developmental function is typical of this section as well. As would be expected, the ordering of functions in the recapitulation reflects that of the exposition.

The following diagram represents the expanded binary principle, including tonal, motivic, and functional elements typical of sonata-allegro forms.

Part A
Exposition

```
| | I ------------. . . . . . . V ---------------------------V | |
| | i ------------. . . . . . . III ----------------------III | |
```

Group 1	Group 2 (3) (etc.)
Phr. Group	Phrase Group(s)
Period	Period(s)
Expository-Trans.	Expository---Term.

Part B

Development	Recapitulation

|| -------------------------V-I -----------. . . . . . . I --------------------------I ||
|| -------------------------V-i -----------. . . . . . . i --------------------------i ||

Derived motives	Group 1	Group 2 (3) (etc.)
Single section	Phr. Group	Phrase Group(s)
Phrase Group	Period	Period(s)
Transitional and/or Developmental	Expository-Trans.	Expository---Term.

NOTE

In minor keys, the movement in the exposition from the tonic to the minor form of the dominant is virtually never encountered.

Alteration of Elements in the Binary Principle

Examples of alterations in one or more of the elements of the expanded binary principle may be found in relatively early examples of the sonata-allegro form. Example 8.3, composed in 1788, illustrates such an alteration.

Example 8.3   Mozart: Sonata in C major, K. 545, I, mm. 1–4, 42–45

The opening phrase of Group 1 in the exposition of this movement is shown in mm. 1–4. The tonic key is firmly established.

Measures 42–45 represent the beginning of the recapitulation. In this case, the reappearance of the original material does *not* coincide with the return of the tonic key. The perception of the design, then, depends upon the elements of motive and function alone.

NOTE

The tonic key is indeed established later in the recapitulation. The tonal principle itself is not violated; rather, the typical interaction of elements of the principle is not present.

It can be seen that the perception of the design of sonata-allegro structures may rely upon the observation of any or all of the elements of the expanded binary principle. Example 8.4 illustrates a relatively common tonal alteration in sonata-allegro structures of the nineteenth century.

Example 8.4   Beethoven: Sonata in C major, Op. 53, I, mm. 1–42

Example 8.4 *(cont.)*

Group 1 in the exposition of this movement is shown in mm. 1–13. In spite of some tonal instability in these measures, the tonic of C is firmly established. The transition, in mm. 14–35, reaches a half-cadence in E minor in m. 29 and is extended to an elided authentic cadence in E major on the downbeat of m. 35. The perception of expository function in the clear periodic structure that follows suggests the beginning of Group 2. The key, however, is not the one normally associated with this section of the exposition. As in the case of the Mozart example, the perception of the design depends upon the recognition of functional elements that are typically encountered in this part of the structure.

NOTE

1. Although a transition at the end of the exposition returns to the dominant harmony in C, the tonal relationships typical of binary structures are abandoned.
2. In the recapitulation, Group 2 appears in A major, but a rapid modulation to C major restores the appropriate tonal relationships.

The perception of sonata-allegro structures in the late nineteenth and the twentieth centuries often depends upon the relationships among elements other than tonality. The recognition of motivic and functional attributes of such movements is essential to the understanding of their structures.

Additional Formal Units

The following formal unit designations, while not integral features of the sonata-allegro structure, occur frequently as additions to many movements.

Introduction.   In some sonata-allegro movements, the exposition is preceded by a section that prepares the movement in various ways. This section is termed the *introduction*.

Example 8.5   Beethoven: Sonata in C minor, Op. 13, I, mm. 1–10

attacca subito il Allegro

In Example 8.5, the ten measures preceding the Allegro are introductory. While no clearly evident attributes characterize all introductory units, this section includes features that are typical of many.

1. The *tempo* is slower than that of the main body of the movement.
2. The *motivic material* is unrelated to the material of the exposition.
3. The *tonal activity* prepares the exposition.
4. The *phrase structure*, tonal activity, and motivic treatment suggest a combination of expository, developmental, and transitional functions.

From these features, at least two traits emerge that typify introductions. First, introductory units are isolated from the main body of the movement by contrasts in readily audible attributes such as tempo, motive, and texture. Second, their tonal activity initially confirms tonic and then emphasizes tonal areas that prepare the opening of the exposition.

Coda.   Many sonata-allegro movements conclude with sections that extend beyond that part of the recapitulation that refers explicitly to structural units found in the exposition. Such units are termed *coda*.

Example 8.6   Beethoven: Sonata in E-flat, Op. 7, mm. 127–136, 307–362

Example 8.6 *(cont.)*

Measures 127–136 show the last part of the closing section of the movement's exposition. The key is B-flat major. The equivalent section in the recapitulation begins in m. 307 in E-flat major and, with modified voicing, continues in the same manner for six measures. In m. 313, however, material is introduced that was not found at the end of the exposition. This material serves to delay the final cadence and to reinforce the tonic key. Thus, mm. 313–362 constitute the coda.

Although codas vary considerably with regard to length and organization, they tend, as this one does, to exhibit the following characteristics.

1. The principal tonality is reaffirmed by passages that emphasize dominant and tonic harmony.
2. The section has some of the attributes associated with developmental function—for example, fragmentation of previously stated themes, absence of clear phrase structure, sudden changes of dynamics, register, and texture.

Sonatina

The term *sonatina* may refer to a relatively short movement in sonata-allegro form in which the main sections that subdivide the structure are present. The term is also commonly applied to binary movements in which the tonal and motivic elements of sonata-allegro form are present, but which lack a development section.

In Example 8.7, the return to the tonic key in Part B occurs only two measures after the end of Part A.

Example 8.7 Mozart: Sonata in F major, K. 332, II, mm. 1–4, 18–22

Measures 1–4 represent the first phrase of the movement, concluding with a half-cadence in the tonic key. Part A concludes on the downbeat of m. 19 with an authentic cadence in F major. In mm. 19–20, B-flat major is reestablished as tonic; and from m. 21 to the end, the material of Part A is recapitulated in the tonic key. In this case, the tonal role of the development section is fulfilled by the two-measure link (mm. 19–20).

NOTE

1. The division between the two parts is not marked by a double bar.
2. In the return to the tonic, the original melody is slightly varied.

EXERCISES

Study the analytical model, and apply the instructions for analysis to each of the pieces that follow.

1. Listen several times to the music provided.

2. On the score, mark the conclusion of each cadence with a bracket, and indicate its type and the key at that point. Use uppercase letters for major keys, lowercase for minor keys.

3. List changes (if any) in tonality, tempo, meter, and so on that create structural phenomena.

4. Describe the organization of Parts A and B. First, answer the following questions individually in note form.

    a.   What are the important structural phenomena?

    b.   What are the key and the cadence schemes?

    c.   How are the structural units organized?

    d.   What is the structural function of each unit?

    e.   How does standard sonata-allegro terminology apply to these units?

Analytical Model   Mozart: Sonata in E-flat major, K. 282, III

Analytical Model *(cont.)*

Part A

Measures 1–8: Phrase group, ending with half-cadence in E-flat major. Expository function (stable tonality). *Group 1.*

Measures 9–15 (downbeat): A continuous section, marked by changes in dynamics and rhythmic content, ending with a half-cadence in B-flat major. Transitional function (modulation, agitated rhythm, rapid changes in dynamics). *Transition.*

Measures 16–35 (downbeat): Contrasting, symmetrical period to m. 23 (downbeat). Measures 24–35 are a contrasting, three-phrase period; first phrase is a variation of the first phrase of previous period; third phrase is a variation of the second. Both periods in B-flat major. Expository function (stable tonality). *Group 2.*

Measures 35–39 (downbeat): Short section ending with authentic cadence in B-flat major. Terminative function (reiterative cadential activity). *Closing of exposition.*

Part B

Measures 40–61: Phrase group to m. 47, marked by changes in dynamics and motive. Section to m. 55, marked by a change in dynamics. Phrase, marked by changes in rhythm and texture, to half-cadence in C minor in m. 59 with extension to m. 61; mm. 60–61 modulate to E-flat major. Developmental function (altered materials from Group 1 and transition; unstable tonality implying keys of F minor, E-flat major, A-flat major, B-flat major, and C minor). *Development.*

Measure 62–end: Essentially the same as exposition except that transition has been altered so that Group 2 and closing appear in E-flat major. Closing has been extended. *Recapitulation.*

The binary principle is expressed in tonal terms in that Part A begins in E-flat major and closes in B-flat major. Part B returns to E-flat major and remains there until its close. Motivically, the recapitulation is strongly tied to the exposition. Functionally, the exposition reflects the principle of two expository sections that establish the important key areas of the movement. Part B exhibits the function of development followed by the mirrored functional design of the exposition. Terminative function closes Parts A and B.

1. C.P.E. Bach: Sonata in F minor (1781), I
   (Wennerstrom, pp. 172–175)

2. Mozart: Sonata in D major, K. 284, I
   (Wennerstrom, pp. 206–211)

3. Beethoven: Sonata in E major, Op. 14, No. 1, I
   (Wennerstrom, pp. 227–232)

4. Haydn: Sonata in E-flat major, Hob. XVI/52, I
   (Burkhart, pp. 166–173)

5. Mozart: Sonata in B-flat major, K. 333, I
   (Burkhart, pp. 206–212)

6. Beethoven: Sonata in F minor, Op. 2, No. 1, I
   (Burkhart, pp. 260–264)

7. Hindemith: Piano Sonata No. 2, I
   (Burkhart, pp. 532–536)

8. C.P.E. Bach: *Prussian Sonata* No. 1 in F major, I
   (Turek, pp. 274–276)

9. Haydn: Sonata in E minor, Hob. 34, I
   (Turek, pp. 289–292)

10. Beethoven: Sonata in C minor, Op. 10, No. 1, III
(Turek, pp. 372–375)

11. Mozart: *Eine kleine Nachtmusik,* I
(Norton Scores I, pp. 480–487)

In addition, the first movements from the majority of Mozart's and Haydn's piano sonatas may profitably be studied.

Some of Beethoven's sonatas are possibly too complex to be investigated at this point. The first movements of the following sonatas, however, are worthy of consideration: Op. 2, No. 2; Op. 10, Nos. 1 and 2; Op. 14, No. 2; Op. 22.

9

the rondo principle

INTRODUCTION

In Chapter 5, the ternary principle was initially defined as one of *statement, contrast, and restatement*. The rondo principle may be viewed as an expansion of the ternary principle insofar as it involves *statement* followed by *alternating contrasts* and *restatements*. Rondo movements, therefore, tend to be perceived in five, seven, or nine (or more) main parts and are labeled A-B-A-B-A, A-B-A-C-A, A-B-A-C-A-B-A, A-B-A-C-A-D-A, and so on, depending upon whether the melodic/thematic material in the contrasting sections is interrelated or not. Part A is commonly called the *refrain* or *ritornello*. Part B is variously designated *couplet, digression, episode,* or *intermezzo,* depending to some extent on the period under investigation. For the sake of clarity, here the refrain will be called the *primary section,* and the contrasting sections will be called *alternating sections.*

Examples 9.1 and 9.2 exemplify the rondo principle in very different ways.

Example 9.1 Adam de la Halle: "Diex soit ne cheste maison." From *Historical*
Anthology of Music, Vol. I. Copyright 1946, 1949 by the
President and Fellows of Harvard College; renewed 1974 by
Alice D. Humez and Willi Apel. Reprinted by permission of
Harvard University Press.

Example 9.1 (from the thirteenth century) shows the rondo principle in both music and text. The short primary section (to the double bar) is stated, and eventually restated twice. It is an eight-measure period. A much longer section follows the first statement and restatement, musical contrast being created largely by an asymmetrical phrase structure articulated every three or four measures by two quarter-note rests; the text is different on each occasion. Thus, the musical organization lends to the structure the label A-B-A-B-A, whereas the text is represented by the label A-B-A-C-A.

Example 9.2 Bartók: *Ten Easy Pieces,* "Evening in the Country" New Version
© Copyright 1950 by Boosey & Hawkes, Inc., New York.
Reprinted by permission.

Example 9.2 *(cont.)*

The rondo principle is equally evident in this short piano piece. There are three statements of the primary section (*Lento, rubato*) and two of the alternating section (*Vivo, non rubato*). The initial primary section, constructed of four short phrases, is varied on each subsequent return. Similarly, the alternating sections, in which the phrase structure is less clearly defined, are variants one of another. Contrast between primary and alternating sections is provided by changes in tempo, rhythm, and dynamics.

Rondo Form

The rondo principle, although exploited extensively in earlier vocal music, was not systematically applied to instrumental music until the middle of the seventeenth century. It may be found, on a relatively large scale, in the *ritornello* movements of the Baroque concerti grossi; these concerti, however, fall outside the scope of this text. On the other hand, in the *rondeau*, an instrumental dance, the principle is easily perceived, as it is in the classical *rondo* that followed it.

The early Baroque rondo (rondeau) shown in Example 9.3 exemplifies the importance of tonal phenomena in creating a contrast between the primary section and alternating sections.

Example 9.3   Purcell: *Abdelazar*, Rondo

Example 9.3 *(cont.)*

In this case, the primary section (Part A) is a single eight-measure phrase closing with an authentic cadence in D minor. Its function is largely expository.

The first alternating section (Part B) begins immediately in F major in m. 9. Despite the motivic similarity between the opening measures of sections A and B, contrast is provided by the clear perception of change of tonality in m. 9. Section B is also an expository eight-measure phrase.

Following a literal repeat of Part A (mm. 17–24), the second alternating section (Part C) establishes the key of A minor. This section is a phrase group of two symmetrical four-measure units. The first cadence is authentic in A minor (m. 28), and thus the expository function of the phrase is established. The second phrase is transitional in function, closing with a half-cadence in D minor that prepares the final statement of the primary section.

The final literal repetition of Part A creates a sectional scheme of A-B-A-C-A, in which the rondo principle is clearly perceived.

NOTE

1. Alternating sections are marked most clearly by the perception of abrupt changes in tonality. The emphasis on tonal rather than dramatic motivic contrasts is typical of Baroque procedure.
2. While all but one of the sections in this example are tonally closed single-phrase units, the rondo principle does not dictate the organization of the various sections.

Example 9.4   Haydn: Sonata in D major, Hob. XVI/37, III

Example 9.4 *(cont.)*

Example 9.4 *(cont.)*

Example 9.4 is constructed of five main sections. The primary section (Part A), mm. 1–20, is in rounded binary form and, in terms of structural units and function, is very similar to Example 4.5, which was also composed by Haydn.

The first alternating section (Part B) is in the parallel minor mode and is also a rounded binary structure (mm. 21–60). Contrast is initially achieved by changes in mode, motive, rhythm, and texture.

Following an exact restatement of A, the second alternating section (Part C) begins in G major. Measures 61–80 constitute yet another rounded binary design, although the nonmodulating period of which the first eight measures are composed weakens the binary principle with respect to tonality. Contrast between Parts C and A is created again by changes in tonality, rhythm, and motive, although a change in texture is not immediately perceived. Measures 81–93 serve to modulate back to D major, arrival at the dominant occurring in m. 87.

The primary section, when it returns in m. 94, differs from the two previous statements. The repeat of the first eight measures (mm. 102–109) is written out in varied form, and the left-hand accompaniment in Part B is more elaborate.

NOTE

Because each section of this example is a clearly articulated rounded binary structure, this rondo is another representation of a *composite form*.

EXERCISES

Apply the instructions for analysis to each of the following pieces.

1. Listen several times to the music provided.

2. On the score, mark the conclusion of each cadence with a bracket, and indicate its type and the key at that point. Use uppercase letters for major keys, lowercase for minor keys.

3. List changes (if any) in tonality, tempo, meter, and so on that create structural phenomena.

4. By identifying the primary and alternating sections and other structural units, describe in a short paragraph how the rondo principle is expressed in this piece of music. First, answer the following questions individually in note form.

    a. What are the important structural phenomena?

    b. What are the key and the cadence schemes?

    c. How are the structural units organized?

    d. What is the structural function of each unit?

    e. What is the structural type of each part?

1. Mozart: *Don Giovanni*, "Mi tradì quell'alma ingrata"
(Wennerstrom, pp. 200–204)

2. Schubert: Incidental Music for the play *Rosamunde* (1823), Entr'acte
(Wennerstrom, pp. 294–297)

3. Couperin: *Pièces de Clavecin*, Sixth Ordre, "Les Baricades mistérieuses"
(Burkhart, pp. 78–81)

4. Haydn: Symphony No. 101 in D major, IV
(Burkhart, pp. 185–194)

5. Beethoven: Sonata in C minor, Op. 13, II
(Norton Scores I, pp. 580–582)

6. Gluck: *Orfeo ed Euridice*, "Che farò senza Euridice"
(Norton Scores I, pp. 309–311)

7. Schumann: *Fantasiestücke*, "Aufschwung"
(Norton Scores II, pp. 217–221)

8. Haydn: Sonata in D major, Hob. XVI/19, III

Sonata-Rondo Form

As has been stated earlier, composite forms are those in which any *part* of a large structure may be clearly identified as representing a separate, complete expression of a structural principle. Composite ternary structures are examples of such forms; so are rondos that contain binary structures as parts of their design.

Sonata-rondo, a common rondo type of the eighteenth and nineteenth centuries, may be considered a hybrid form, in which tonal, motivic, or functional principles characteristic of sonata-allegro structures are integrated into a basic rondo design.

Example 9.5, though labeled "Rondo" by the composer, includes several tonal and functional features associated with the binary principle in sonata-allegro form.

Example 9.5   Beethoven: Sonata in D major, Op. 28, IV

Example 9.5 *(cont.)*

Example 9.5 *(cont.)*

Example 9.5 *(cont.)*

Example 9.5 *(cont.)*

The main sections of this seven-part rondo are perceived as follows.

Part A: mm. 1–28 (Primary Section)

Part A begins with an expository group of four phrases that reaches a perfect authentic cadence on the downbeat of m. 16. Measure 17, marked by increased rhythmic activity, initiates a transition in which a modulation to the dominant takes place, concluding with a half-cadence in A major in m. 28.

Part B: mm. 29–50 (Alternating Section)

Part B, like Part A, is divided into two distinct sections. It begins with an extended group of three phrases in A major (mm. 29–43), which may be perceived as partially developmental motivically. Tonally, however, the group is expository in function. Its final cadence, on the downbeat of m. 43, is elided with the second section, mm. 43–50, which is initially terminative in function. The last four measures, however, effect a modulation back to the tonic to prepare for the return of Part A in m. 51.

NOTE

The music through the downbeat of m. 47 is perceived tonally, motivically, and functionally, precisely as the exposition of a typical sonata-allegro structure would be.

Part A: mm. 51–67 (Primary Section)

This section is an embellished restatement of the first expository phrase group (mm. 1–17).

Part C: mm. 68–113 (Alternating Section)

This part begins in D major, but by m. 75 G major is established, and the activity is tonally expository in that key through the downbeat of m. 87. Motivically, however, the music is clearly developmental, using altered versions of the motives from the initial primary section. The music from m. 87 to the downbeat of m. 101 is both tonally and motivically developmental, concluding with a half-cadence in D minor. From m. 101 to the downbeat of m. 113 a dominant pedal prevails, and the only tonal activity is a modal change from D minor to D major. The motivic activity, however, is developmental.

NOTE

Part C lacks much of the contrast normally associated with alternating sections of rondo structures. In fact, tonally, motivically, and functionally, it is precisely analogous to the development section of a typical sonata-allegro structure.

Part A: mm. 114–144 (Primary Section)

This section is similar to the original primary section, although slightly longer. It is once again divided into two discrete parts. Measures 114–129 are almost identical to the first sixteen measures of the movement; the remainder of the section exploits the same rhythmic figurations that at first served as a transition to the dominant key. Here, however, there is no *real* transition, for the music remains in the tonic throughout and comes to rest on the dominant note on the downbeat of m. 144.

NOTE

The increased chromatic activity in mm. 130–144 (compared with mm. 17–28) that extends this "transitional" section serves to prepare the key of D major as if it were a new tonality. The function of this section is similar to that of the transition between Group 1 and Group 2 in the recapitulation of sonata-allegro forms.

Part B: mm. 145–168 (Alternating Section)

This part is essentially a repeat of the first alternating section (mm. 29–50) *in the tonic key*. It is a single measure longer.

NOTE

The tonal, motivic, and functional attributes of the music in mm. 114–168 are precisely those of the recapitulation of a sonata-allegro structure whose exposition shares the tonal relationship of the original Parts A and B of this rondo movement.

Part A: mm. 169–192 (Primary Section)

The music from mm. 169–192 is perceived tonally in three units. The first phrase (mm. 169–172), in G major, is a simplification of the first phrase of the movement. The second phrase (mm. 173–177) begins in the same manner but concludes with a half-cadence in D major on the downbeat of m. 177. It is tonally transitional in function. Measures 177–192 represent a dominant pedal and may be perceived tonally as a prolongation of the half-cadence in m. 177.

Coda: m..193–end

This entire section, isolated from the rest of the movement by the fermata in m. 192 and by a change in tempo, may properly be termed *coda*. However, in terms of bass line and harmony, the first eight measures consist of a restatement of the first two phrases of Part A in D major, and thus serve as the final return of the beginning of the primary section. The remainder of the music is cadential in nature, providing the coda's predictable terminative function at the end.

Summary

In Example 9.5, the principle of alternating statements, contrasts, and restatements clearly governs the organization of the movement. The parts may be labeled A-B-A-C(development)-A-B-A(coda). As noted earlier, tonal and functional attributes associated with these sections suggest a strong relationship with attributes associated with sonata-allegro movements. More important, the highly sectional contrasting nature of the rondo principle has been, in part, replaced by the developmental nature of typical binary movements.

The following diagram compares the elements of typical sonata-allegro and sonata-rondo forms, and illustrates the way in which the elements of the principles are combined.

Sonata-Allegro (Binary)

```
Part A                              Part B
Exposition                          Development         Recapitulation
I ------. . . . V ----------------V ||  ------------------------------V-I ------. . . . I --------------------I
i ------. . . . III --------------III ||  ------------------------------V-i ------. . . . i --------------------i
Gr.1        Gr.2                    M.M.                Gr.1        Gr.2
```

Sonata-Rondo (Sectional)

```
A        B        A        C                                    A        B        A
I ------I . . . V ------. . . I ------I . . .  ------------------------------V-I ------I . . . I ------. . . I ------I
i -------i . . . III ----. . . i -------i . . .  ------------------------------V-i -------i . . . i -------. . . i -------i
P.S.      A.S.      P.S.      M.M.                                P.S.      A.S.      P.S.
```

Gr.1 = Group 1
Gr.2 = Group 2
M.M. = Motivic Manipulation
P.S. = Primary Section
A.S. = Alternating Section

To summarize, in the sonata-rondo, after the first return of the primary section, the remaining sections follow the tonal and functional relationships as the tonal and motivic *result* of the opening sections. Were it not for the first restatement of Part A, the structure would be perceived as being governed by the binary principle.

EXERCISES

Follow the instructions for the exercises earlier in the chapter. In addition, describe how elements of the binary principle interact with those of the rondo principle.

1. Beethoven: Sonata in E major, Op. 14, No. 1, III
   (Wennerstrom, pp. 235–239)

2. Mozart: Sonata in B-flat major, K. 333, III
   (Burkhart, pp. 215–220)

3. Beethoven: Sonata in C minor, Op. 13, III
   (Burkhart, pp. 275–281; Norton Scores I, pp. 583–588)

4. Mozart: Sonata in B-flat major, K. 281, III

5. Beethoven: Sonata in A major, Op. 2, No. 2, IV

6. Beethoven: Sonata in G major, Op. 31, No. 1, III

10

atypical formal organization

INTRODUCTION

Formal analysis begins with the perception of structural divisions as marked by structural phenomena. An investigation of the functional qualities of, and the relationships among, these divisions may lead to the discovery of fundamental organizing principles. So far in this text, standard formal labels have been applied to the pieces of music that have been studied. Such labeling is appropriate because those pieces are representative of a large number of similar expressions of the various organizing principles. For example, *rounded binary form* describes large numbers of movements that share the tonal, motivic, and functional elements peculiar to that expression of the binary principle.

There are, however, many pieces of music whose structural divisions are organized so that the application of standard formal labels or the identification of organizing principles is problematic. In this chapter, a number of pieces will be discussed that represent atypical formal organization on one or more levels, and suggestions for describing their structures will be made. It must be stressed that such works are subject to the same analytical procedures as those studied in Chapters 4 through 9, although the outcome of the analyses may depend upon a more flexible interpretation of the elements of the organizing principles than has previously been required.

Examples for Study

Example 10.1 is a piece of music that clearly adheres to a single organizing principle but whose internal relationships are such that the application of a standard formal label is not appropriate.

Example 10.1 Haydn: Sonata in E-flat major, II

Example 10.1 *(cont.)*

This movement is perceived in two large sections, clearly marked by important cadences in mm. 23 and 56 (visually reinforced by the double bars). Further, because Part A is tonally open and because Part B is motivically related to it, the two parts may be said to be interdependent. Thus, the fundamental conditions necessary for the perception of the binary principle (first stated in Chapter 4) are fulfilled, and the movement may be described as a clear expression of that principle.

Part A begins with a four-measure expository phrase in C minor, followed by another four-measure phrase, which concludes with a perfect authentic cadence in G minor. The two phrases form a phrase group, the second phrase of which is partially transitional in function.

Measures 8–19 constitute a section, motivically distinct from the opening phrases, that at first confirms the G minor tonality and then modulates to B-flat major, ending with a perfect authentic cadence on the downbeat of m. 19. Measures 19–23 represent a section with terminative function, closing with a perfect authentic cadence in B-flat major.

Measures 24–41 are developmental in function and are motivically related to the opening phrase group of the movement. These measures are divided into two sections, the first of which concludes with a half-cadence in G minor in m. 31 and the second with a half-cadence in C minor in m. 41.

From m. 41 to m. 48, the musical activity is closely related motivically to mm. 9–19. This section, however, is tonally stable in C minor and exhibits expository and terminative function. Measures 48–52 are a transposition of mm. 19–23. The movement closes with a varied repetition of mm. 1–4.

It is necessary to compare the elements of this movement's design with those of the standard expressions of the binary principle in order to determine whether a standard formal label is applicable. A comparison, therefore, of the tonal, functional, and motivic attributes of this piece with those of typical simple, rounded, and sonata-allegro binary structures follows.

Tonality.   The key signature of this piece suggests a tonality of G minor, and indeed, with the exception of the first two phrases, Part A exhibits the tonal organization associated with that key. With the return of the tonic key in m. 41, however, Part B displays a tonal scheme typical of a binary structure in the key of C minor, thus confirming the tonality of the opening phrase of the movement. This movement, then, does not reflect the key scheme of typical binary structures. Further, the presence of three established keys in Part A suggests a more complex tonal organization than is normally associated with movements in simple or rounded binary form.

Motive. The music is based primarily on three discrete motivic ideas, associated respectively with the first phrase group (mm. 1–8), the transitional section (mm. 8–19), and the terminative section (mm. 19–23) of Part A. Such motivic complexity is atypical of simple or rounded binary forms, but not unusual in sonata-allegro structures. In Part B, the return of the first motivic idea does not coincide with the return of the tonic key; thus, the procedure is not typical of either rounded binary or sonata-allegro structures.

Function. Functionally, the organization of the movement more closely resembles that of sonata-allegro form than that of the simpler binary structures. The absence, however, of clear expository function in the final key area of Part A, and of a transitional section in Part B, weakens the perception of sonata-allegro form.

Conclusion. Although the movement clearly expresses the binary principle, it has been shown that in terms of tonality, motive, and function, it fits comfortably none of the standard formal designations associated with the principle. In terms of the application of a formal label, it can be said, therefore, only that this movement is a "sonata-allegro-like" structure with several irregularities.

In Example 10.2, a single organizing principle is not so clearly expressed.

Example 10.2 Debussy: Preludes, Book 1, "La fille aux cheveux de lin"

Example 10.2 *(cont.)*

The first section of the prelude, a three-phrase group, is contained in mm. 1–11. The first phrase closes with a plagal cadence on the tonic of G-flat in m. 3 and is expository in function. The second phrase, ending with an authentic cadence on E-flat in m. 6, is partially transitional in function. The final phrase of the group is a varied restatement of the first, ending with an authentic cadence in m. 10. This cadence is extended through m. 11. A change in tempo defines the end of the first section and the beginning of the next.

The second section consists of a single phrase that, after a strong tonicization of the subdominant in m. 16, suggests terminative function in the tonic in m. 17 and the downbeat of m. 18. The B-flat dominant perfect eleventh chord in the remainder of m. 18 serves primarily to introduce the E-flat tonality of the following section. The motivic material of this section is related to that of the first, and the function is largely expository.

The third section, marked by a change in tempo and by increased rhythmic activity, begins in m. 19. It is a single phrase whose tonal center shifts from E-flat in mm. 19–21 to A-flat in m. 22. A change in tempo in m. 23 marks the end of the section, the last chord of which effects a modulation to G-flat. The function is perceived as both expository and transitional.

The fourth section, marked by a change in texture, is a phrase consisting of a two-measure unit in mm. 24–25 that is repeated and varied in mm. 26–27. Each two-measure unit concludes with the dominant harmony in G-flat, though in neither case is a half-cadence perceived. The tonal center of G-flat is felt more strongly in the second half of the section, but the function is mainly expository or terminative. Motivically, the music is related to the opening phrase of the prelude. A change in tempo again marks the end of the section.

The first chord of the final section (mm. 28–39), a C-flat major triad, is perceived as an evaded resolution of the dominant triad that concludes the previous section. The first phrase of the section contains a repetition of the melody of the opening phrase, extended through augmentation of its cadential figure and accompanied by subdominant, submediant, and tonic harmonies. The tonic chord in m. 32 is perceived as cadential, therefore, primarily through melodic and rhythmic activity. The prelude concludes with a terminative phrase whose opening measures (mm. 33–34) are a repetition and an extension of m. 14.

The grouping of the sections just delineated into larger structural units is necessary so that an overall organization for the prelude can be perceived. This process, again, depends upon an investigation of the tonal, motivic, and functional elements of the design.

Tonality.   The initial large grouping suggested by tonal elements includes the first two sections of the prelude (mm. 1–18). The prevailing tonal center of G-flat throughout reinforces their perception as a single larger unit. The shifting tonal centers of mm. 19–23, particularly when compared to the stable tonality that follows, define that section as a single unit. However, because the return of the G-flat tonality is more convincing in m. 28, the section from mm. 24–27 may be grouped with mm. 19–23 in terms of tonal instability. The remaining section is another single unit.

The tonal relationships among these units may suggest the consideration of two organizing principles. Because the B-flat dominant eleventh chord in m. 18 establishes no new tonality in the first section, the section is perceived as tonally closed, although no cadential activity involving the tonic is present. The corresponding return of a stable G-flat tonality later in the piece suggests a ternary tonal organization. However, the tonal instability of the second large section is more typical of binary structures.

Motive.   Most of the music in the first two sections (mm. 1–18) is based on melodic and rhythmic motives found in the opening phrase of the prelude. Measures 19–23, however, are not so clearly defined in terms of the original motivic content. Measures 19–21 are derived from mm. 15–16, while the music in mm. 22–23 is less obviously related to motivic ideas previously heard. The music from mm. 24–27 is based on the arpeggiated E-flat minor seventh chord with which the prelude begins. The final section (mm. 28–39) is essentially a restatement of motivic ideas presented in the first eighteen measures.

In terms of motivic activity, therefore, the prelude may be perceived in three large sections, the first and third (mm. 1–18 and mm. 28–39) based specifically on the same motivic ideas, and the second (mm. 19–27) loosely derived from those ideas or exposing new ones. While the new motivic material in the second large section may suggest a ternary organization, the same material may be perceived as an outgrowth of that from mm. 1–18, thus suggesting a rounded binary form.

Function.   The first two sections of the prelude (mm. 1–18) are unified by function as well as by tonality and motive. They exhibit primarily expository function throughout. Measures 19–23 are both transitional and developmental in function. Measures 24–27, however, are tonally expository but motivically developmental. The function of this section, therefore, is somewhat unclear. The remaining measures are expository and terminative.

Because of the developmental nature of mm. 19–27, a binary functional organization is suggested. The absence, however, of transitional function at the end of the first large section weakens the perception of interdependence, upon which the binary principle is based.

Conclusion.   The assignment of either binary or ternary labels to this prelude essentially depends upon the perception of the second large section (mm. 19–27). If the section is fundamentally perceived as a contrast to the first section, then a ternary interpretation is appropriate. If, on the other hand, the section is perceived as an outgrowth of the first, the prelude more closely resembles a rounded binary structure. The preceding analysis has demonstrated that in some respects neither interpretation describes the prelude's organization accurately. It can be said, therefore, that the piece has attributes of both binary and ternary design.

The structure of Example 10.3 produces a composite design with several unusual features.

Example 10.3   Field: Nocturnes, No. 13 in D minor

Example 10.3 *(cont.)*

The first obvious division in this nocturne occurs in m. 32, in which there is a change in mode. The music to that point represents a rounded binary structure. Part A begins with an eight-measure period that modulates from D minor to F major in the second phrase. The period is followed by a four-measure terminative section in F major. The tonal and functional attributes of this section are typical of binary structures. Part B (beginning with the anacrusis to m. 13) opens with a developmental and transitional phrase ending with a half-cadence in D minor in m. 16. Measures 17–20 are a varied repetition of the first phrase of the piece, concluding with a perfect authentic cadence in D minor, thus confirming the rounded binary structure. Measures 21–28 represent a varied repetition of mm. 13–20, followed by a four-measure terminative section that is a transposition of the last four measures of Part A (mm. 9–12).

The second major section of the nocturne, in D major, begins with a double period consisting of two pairs of contrasting antecedent and consequent four-measure phrases (mm. 33–40 and mm. 41–48). Measures 49–56 represent a contrasting period. The first phrase concludes with an imperfect authentic cadence in m. 52, the second with a perfect authentic cadence in m. 56. The two phrases of the period are an embellished repetition of the first two phrases of the double period that opens the D major section. Measures 57–69 are a phrase group. In m. 57, a varied repetition of the first phrase of the preceding period begins. The concluding figure of the phrase, expected on the anacrusis to m. 60, is replaced by the introductory figure of a phrase in D minor that begins in that measure; thus, the two phrases are elided. The second phrase and the six measures that follow it are a varied repetition and an extension of the last eight measures of the first large section of the nocturne.

The internal structures of both major divisions of this nocturne are clear. The first large section is comfortably described as a rounded binary structure. The second large section, however, can be labeled only with reference to its period and phrase group structures and the relationships between them. Because the first large section is a rounded binary form, the complete movement may be described as a composite form.

The *principle* that governs the relationship between the two large sections is not immediately apparent, although the *details* of the relationship in terms of tonality, motive, and function are easily described.

Tonality.   The first large section is tonally closed in D minor. The second, in D major through m. 59, returns to the original tonality in m. 60. In terms of tonality, then, a ternary organization is suggested, although the brevity of the musical activity in D minor at the end weakens the perception of a three-part design.

Motive.   The two large divisions of the nocturne are obviously related by motive. Indeed, almost all the music in the piece is motivically derived from the melodic and rhythmic activity found in the opening phrase. Because mm. 60–69 are directly related to mm. 25–32, again a weak ternary organization may be suggested. The overall motivic organization of the piece, however, is not typical of ternary structures.

Function.   The fact that the first section is a rounded binary structure defines its functional attributes clearly. The second large section, including the closing measures in D minor, is almost exclusively expository in function. Thus, unless a purely motivic developmental relationship between the parts is perceived, function plays a minor role in describing the relationship between them.

Conclusion. A ternary description of the nocturne is possible in terms of tonality and motive. However, the elision of the phrase beginning in m. 60 in D minor with the phrase that precedes it makes the perception of the concluding D minor section as a discrete unit problematic. Because of clear motivic relationships, the second large section may be perceived as an outgrowth of the first; thus, a binary interpretation is also possible. The second section, however, has none of the typical functional attributes associated with second parts of binary forms.

As in the case of the Debussy prelude analyzed earlier, neither a binary nor a ternary interpretation of the design accurately describes the nocturne's organization. The most that can be said is that this is a composite structure in two large sections whose relationships on all levels prevent the ready identification of its organizing principle. Unlike the Debussy prelude, then, to which either of two labels may be applied, no standard formal label seems appropriate for the Field nocturne. Had the D minor section at the end of the piece contained a more nearly complete return of the opening section, the term *composite ternary form* would describe the structure accurately. *Incomplete ternary form,* then, may be an appropriate label for the structure.

EXERCISES

The analyses of the pieces in this chapter provide a model approach to the analyses of similar structures of unusual organization or to the analysis of any piece of music that is unfamiliar. The procedure, outlined here, may be described as a series of steps with several alternative conclusions.

1. Describe the structural divisions as perceived through structural phenomena.

2. Provide a complete tonal, motivic, and functional analysis of the relationships among those divisions.

3. Compare the relationships among the *largest* structural units with those that typically define commonly used organizing principles.

4a. If the structure may be described comfortably as an expression of a single organizing principle, describe the tonal, motivic, and functional relationships among the smaller units of the structure.

4b. If more than one principle seems to describe the organization of the structure, describe the attributes of organization that most closely resemble those of the principles involved. Describe the tonal, motivic, and functional relationships among the smaller units of the structure.

4c. If no principle or combination of principles describes the structure accurately, describe the relationships among the larger structural units as completely as possible. Describe the tonal, motivic, and functional relationships among the smaller units of the structure.

5a. Apply a standard formal label, such as *rounded binary,* to the structure if the relationships among the smaller structural units are typical of such expressions of an organizing principle. If those relationships are atypical, describe forms or procedures that the structure most closely resembles.

5b. In the case of 4b or 4c, describe attributes that resemble those of standard formal types, or apply terminology that compares the structure to such forms.

Following the preceding procedure, provide a complete analysis of each piece listed here.

1. Chopin: Preludes, Op. 28, No. 21 in B-flat major (Wennerstrom, pp. 338–339)

2. Debussy: Preludes, Book II, "Canope" (Wennerstrom, pp. 411–413)

3. Hindemith: *Ludus Tonalis,* "Interludium" (Wennerstrom, pp. 496–497)

4. Beethoven: Sonata in A major, Op. 101, I (Burkhart, pp. 310–312)

5. Chopin: Mazurka in B-flat major, Op. 7, No. 1 (Burkhart, pp. 360–361)

6. Schoenberg: Three Piano Pieces, Op. 11, No. 1 (Burkhart, pp. 455–458)

7. C.P.E. Bach: *Prussian Sonata* No. 1 in F major, Andante (Turek, pp. 276–277)

8. Chopin: Preludes, Op. 28, No. 21 in B-flat major (Turek, pp. 496–498)

9. Schoenberg: Klavierstücke, Op. 33a (Turek, pp. 763–767)

10. Field: Nocturnes, No. 3 in A-flat major

11. Liszt: Vier kleine Klavierstücke (1865), II

12. Debussy: *Suite bergamasque*, Passapied

13. Milhaud: *Household Muse*, "The Cat"

14. Bernstein: *Four Anniversaries*, "for Felicia Montealegre"

index of musical examples

index

A

Alternating section, 170
Answer:
  real, 112
  tonal, 112
Antecedent phrase, 34
Asymmetrical period, 38, 47
Atypical organization, 195, 210
Augmentation, 102, 115

B

Basso ostinato, 126
Binary form:
  rounded, 71–74
  simple, 64–67
Binary principle, 61–75
  alteration of elements, 154–57
  elements of, 63–64
  in rounded binary form, 74
  in simple binary form, 68
  in sonata-allegro form, 153–54

C

Cadence as structural phenomenon, 2–5
Cadential extension, 38, 47, 104
Cantus firmus, 121
Chaconne, 126, 131
Closed section, 83
Closing section, 47
  in fugue, 108
  in sonata-allegro form, 151–52
Coda, 159–62
Composite form, 91, 181, 182
Composite ternary form, 91–93, 182
Consequent phrase, 34
Continuous variations, 126–32
Contraction, 102, 115
Contrapuntal texture, 96
Contrasting period, 37, 47
Countersubject, 113
Couplet, 170

D

Density as structural phenomenon, 15–18
Development, 151–52